AUTHENTIC MODEL RAILWAY
OPERATION

BY

MARTIN NIELD

WILD SWAN BOOKS LTD.

CONTENTS

WILD SWAN BOOKS LTD.

© 2016 Wild Swan Books Ltd and Martin Nield

ISBN 978-1-912038-00-8

Designed by Paul Karau
Printed by Amadeus Press Ltd., Cleckheaton

Published by
Wild Swan Books Ltd
3A Upper Lambridge Street, Bath, BA1 6RY

Preface

Towards the end of the afternoon, the goods yard pilot at Croston Sidings collects a brake van from one of the sidings and whistles to the signalman, seeking permission to cross the Preston-Liverpool main line and head down the branch line to Eccleston.

The Croston Sidings signalman and the signalman at Eccleston agree this move by sending and receiving the appropriate bell codes and the Eccleston signalman confirms what they have agreed by changing the position of the down line block instrument from Line Blocked to Line Clear. This indication is also repeated in the Croston Sidings signal box.

Once these actions have been completed, the Croston Sidings signalman can lower his branch starting signal, giving the driver of the goods yard pilot permission to begin his journey.

As the loco and brake van pass the signal box, the Croston Sidings signalman will glance out to ensure he can see the tail light on the brake van and then he will send a message to the Eccleston signalman to tell him the train is entering the block section. The Eccleston signalman will acknowledge the signal and switch his down line block instrument to Train on Line. Once again this indication is also repeated in the Croston Sidings signal box. When the train has disappeared from sight, the Croston Sidings signalman will restore his branch starting signal to danger.

A few minutes later the loco and brake van will approach the terminus at Eccleston. As the loco and brake van are only loose-coupled (i.e. not vacuum braked), they will be brought to a stand at the home signal. Once the Eccleston signalman is certain that the train is under control, he will lower his home signal giving permission for the loco and brake van to enter the station. When the loco and brake van have passed the signal box and the signalman has confirmed the train is complete by checking the tail lamp, he will send a message to the signalman at Croston Sidings saying the train is now out of the block section, restore his block instrument to Line Blocked and restore his home signal to danger.

And so a simple move of a loco and brake van from one place to another is completed. What a fascinating process! This is what would have happened in real life and so – if we are to make authentic and realistic model railways – this is what we should do on our layouts. However, most model railway layouts, especially those which appear at exhibitions, do not operate like this. Locomotives reverse in an instant, propel coaches to which they are not attached, and pass signals (where they exist!) at danger with impunity. These and many other transgressions of the rules of real railway operation destroy the illusion of reality for observers at an exhibition and display an unfortunate lack of knowledge on the part of the layout operators about how real railways work.

However, this is not going to be a book of 'thou shalt not' and rules which must be obeyed. Rather it is hopefully going to be a book which demonstrates how much more enjoyable it is to operate a model railway authentically. Many modellers derive enormous pleasure from the creation of accurate model locomotives, carriages, wagons, buildings and scenery. My aim in writing this book is to persuade

A signalman sets the road for a train. This is the interior of Ramsbottom signal box on the East Lancashire Railway. AUTHOR

The Eccleston branch Pilot Goods loco, L&YR Barton Wright 0-6-0 No. 952, arrives at Eccleston with a brake van ready to shunt the yard and form a return working to Croston Sidings.
SIMON EDMUNDS

Where it all started for me – Preston station in the 1960s. In this remarkable photograph taken on 24th August 1962, Peter Fitton has captured two Jubilees running into the station at the same time. On the left No. 45710 *Irresistible* was running into what was Platform 5 with the 4.25 Manchester Victoria to Blackpool, while on the right No. 45713 *Renown* was running into the former Platform 4 with a Liverpool to Glasgow train.   PETER FITTON

Ex-LMS 'Jinty' 0-6-0 No. 47472 acting as a station pilot at Preston in the 1960s. It was removing the empty stock of a train which had recently arrived from Wigan.   RAIL ONLINE

Fort William was one of my favourite locations to watch trains during family holidays in Scotland in the 1960s. Steam had gone by the time I got there, but the methods of working had not changed. In this photo from the 1950s K1 2-6-0 No. 62031 was setting off from Fort William with a passenger train. The signalman is seen preparing to hand over the token for the single-line section to Mallaig Junction.
        RAIL ONLINE

them that they can add an extra dimension to their hobby by understanding real railway operation and striving to reproduce it in miniature. Operating a model railway in accordance with prototype practice is fun!

My interest in railway operation started soon after I began train spotting near my home in Preston in the early 1960s. Along with many school friends, I began by watching trains go by on the busy West Coast Main Line. There was a glorious procession of trains from expresses hauled by Duchesses and Britannia Pacifics to local passenger trains hauled by 2-6-4T tanks and, of course, a huge variety of freight traffic. Taking engine numbers was fun, but I soon began to wonder where all these trains were coming from and where they were going to.

Later we moved our vantage point to the south end of Preston station from where we could see the same procession of trains, but also observe the comings and goings of the station pilot (usually 'Jinty' No. 47472) and the endless shunting in the adjacent goods yards. I began to wonder what all this shunting was about and why some types of locomotive were used to haul some types of train, but not others. And then, of course, there was also the wonderful display of mechanical signalling controlling everything. But why were there so many signal boxes and what did they all do?

Around the same time we began to have family holidays in Scotland, starting with two years in succession at Pitlochry on the Highland main line. My indulgent parents (I was an only child) were happy to leave me for hours on Pitlochry station while they went off enjoying the sights. During those holidays I was able to observe at close quarters the passing of trains and the exchange of tokens in the station and the shunting of the morning pick-up goods. Unfortunately, by this time (1964/5) the trains were diesel-hauled, but I doubt if the methods of working had changed much in the preceding 50 years.

Over the next few years I was able to explore further afield from my Preston home, riding my bike to Lostock Hall to visit the engine shed but also to watch the shunting in the nearby yards. And on the family summer holidays I saw train working at Fort William, Mallaig, Oban and Kyle of Lochalsh.

At home I was reading model railway magazines like *Railway Modeller* and *Model Railway Constructor*. Articles in these magazines also inspired me and I still occasionally re-read classic articles from the 1960s such as David Jenkinson's articles about his layouts 'Marthwaite' and 'Garsdale Road'; Peter Denny's articles about his 'Buckingham' branch; or Frank Dyer's articles about his layout 'Borchester'. And I began to go to model railway exhibitions, such as the famous Manchester Christmas shows in the Corn Exchange, where I saw many inspiring layouts such as 'Presson' – a pioneering EM gauge branch terminus.

All these childhood experiences made a profound impact upon me and provided me with many happy memories. They have also been my inspiration on my journey to discover more about railway operation. I hope you enjoy

Two inspirational editions of Railway Modeller *from the 1960s featuring David Jenkinson's 'Marthwaite' and Peter Denny's 'Grandborough Junction'.*

'Presson', a pioneering EM gauge layout built by John Langan of the Manchester Model Railway Society and exhibited at the famous Christmas shows at the Corn Exchange.

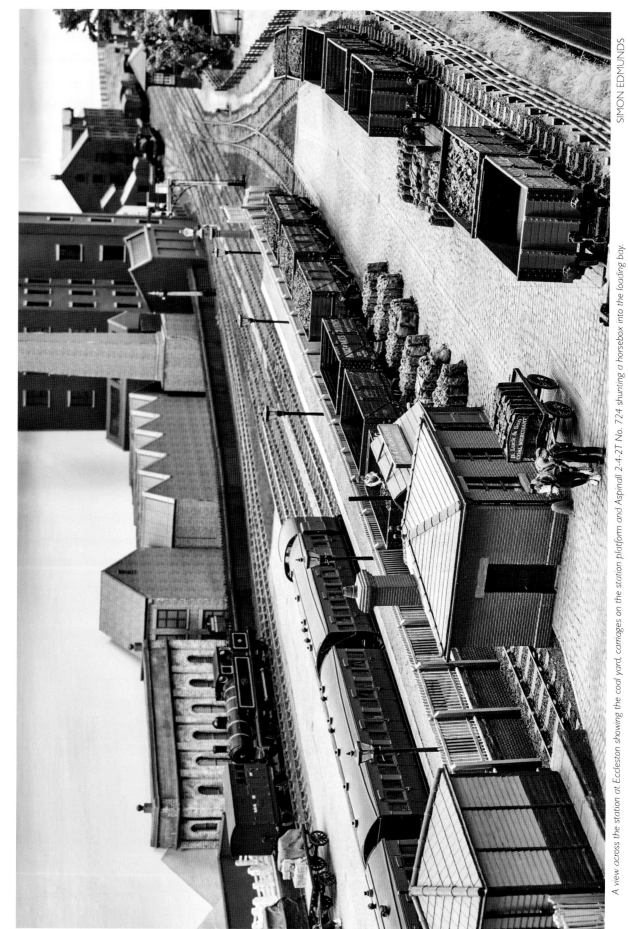

A view across the station at Eccleston showing the coal yard, carriages on the station platform and Aspinall 2-4-2T No. 724 shunting a horsebox into the loading bay.

SIMON EDMUNDS

reading this book and that it encourages you to operate your own layout more realistically.

Of course, there are many more recent layouts which do operate correctly and they have also inspired me. Examples include Chris Pendlenton's wonderful 'North Shields' and Bob Essery's S7 layout 'Dewsbury' and its subsequent spin-offs 'Ellerton Road' and 'Dewsbury Goods'.

Before we go any further, I should explain that this book will be about how the traditional steam railway worked and how to reproduce that in model form. However, many of the principles of railway operation which were established in the steam era continue to this day in the operation of the modern railway using diesel and electric traction. So I hope this book will appeal to all those railway modellers who wish to operate their layouts in a more authentic fashion.

Over the past thirty years or so I have been modelling the Lancashire and Yorkshire Railway (L&YR) in the Pre-Grouping era. I have also been Secretary of The Lancashire and Yorkshire Railway Society (L&YRS) since 2000. For these reasons many of the examples and illustrations I have used in this book are of L&YR origin. I have tried to include examples and photographs from other companies, but when writing a book like this it is best to stick with what you know and so the L&YR will probably predominate.

Over the same period of time I have been involved in building two Scalefour layouts which will also feature prominently in the following pages. The first is my own layout 'Eccleston' which is an L&YR branch terminus set in West Lancashire; the second was 'Calder Bridge', a sizeable

North Eastern Railway (NER) terminus set in West Yorkshire which featured L&YR running powers. 'Calder Bridge' was a joint project built by members of the Newcastle and District Model Railway Society (of which I used to be a member) and featured in *Model Railway Journal* No. 114. It was widely exhibited between 1995 and 2000, but then sold. I will be using these two layouts as the main examples of my approach to authentic model railway operation throughout this book.

One thing they share is their Pre-Grouping time period, but I would like to stress that I am interested in all periods of traditional steam railway operation – Pre-Grouping, Grouping and British Railways. Once the principles of railway operation had been established in the late 19th century they did not change greatly until the 1960s.

There have been a number of books written about model railway operation over the years. Mainly these have covered topics such as how to wire your layout and what sort of couplings to use. There have also been books about how the real railway worked, most notably a very useful series by Bob Essery. Details of these books can be found in the bibliography on page 59.

My approach in the following chapters is a marriage of these two types of book. Each chapter (except the one on exhibition operation) is divided into two sections: *What did the real railway do?* and *How can we replicate this in model form?* The intention is to start – as we always should – with the prototype and then work out how best to reproduce this on our layouts. I hope you find it interesting and that it will lead you to plan authentic operation into your next layout.

Aspinall 0-6-0ST No. 753 runs into Calder Bridge with a loaded mineral train destined for the local gas works.

BARRY NORMAN

Railway work was hard. This wonderfully evocative photo shows ex-L&YR Aspinall 0-6-0 No. 52275 shunting at Royton Junction sidings, near Oldham, on 23rd March 1961. I would love to model a scene like this one day.

RAIL ONLINE

Black Five No. 45275 powers through Great Harwood Junction, near Blackburn, on 29th May 1967 hauling a diesel multiple unit set, an unusual move which would make an interesting feature on a layout set in the era of transition between steam and diesel traction. This picture shows the signals off for trains in both directions and a cross on the water tank which indicated it had been condemned.

LYRS COLLECTION

INTRODUCTION

L&YR Aspinall 2-4-2T No. 724 arrives at Eccleston with an ordinary passenger train from Preston. Here is clear evidence that the camera never lies: the loco needs headlamps, the carriages need lettering and the buildings behind need replacing. These are all jobs on the To Do list! SIMON EDMUNDS

Real railways began with the aim of moving goods (and later passengers) between A and B in the most efficient manner possible. They were built and operated by private companies seeking to maximise their profits. They were not built so that more than a century later thousands of people could enjoy a satisfying hobby studying them!

As railways developed during the 19th and early 20th centuries they became the dominant method of transport in the UK. In the days before the development of the internal combustion engine, their only rivals were horse-drawn road transport or water-borne transport on rivers, canals and coastal waters.

As they developed, they devised methods of operation which enabled them to deliver the services their customers required and to do so safely. Indeed safety became a prominent feature of railway operation, with great emphasis being placed on working within rules and regulations and to complex signalling systems. The story of how these systems developed has been told elsewhere (see Bibliography) but the railway companies learned from major accidents, like that at Armagh in June 1889 which led to the Regulation of Railways Act requiring the use of continuous brakes for passenger carriages, interlocking of points and signals and block section working. The act empowered the Board of Trade to ensure that all railway companies complied with the new safer regime.

Railway work was hard and could be dangerous too. The daily grind of moving the traffic often involved long hours in what today we would regard as primitive conditions; just think of those early steam locomotives with no cabs, or raking out the ashpans at the end of a long shift. Enthusiasts tend to glamorize railway work and, of course, the elite drivers of famous express trains and the Station Master in his frock coat were glamorous occupations. But we should not forget that the fundamental purpose of all this was to shift the coal to the docks, the fish to the market and the commuters to their offices.

When it comes to reproducing this in model form, we need to try and capture this sense of purpose. Simply moving trains around aimlessly or because you have not run a goods train for a while may be enjoyable, but it is not what the real railway did! Most modellers, especially those who follow the 'finescale' approach to the hobby in their chosen scale/gauge combination, put a lot of effort into getting the detailing and painting correct on their latest locomotive or carriage, but, generally speaking, they pay much less attention to making their models work in a railwaylike way.

Realistic operation is not only more authentic, it is also more enjoyable. It gives a purpose to each train movement and, if it involves co-operation between more than one operator, involves teamwork which can be very satisfying. The development of modern digital control systems is leading to more layouts being operated by drivers and signalmen – just like the real thing – which is a sign of progress towards more realistic operation.

Working to a planned timetable means all the team members know what they are supposed to be doing and avoids confusion. This can be very satisfying when working on a complex private layout like 'Castle Rackrent', Richard

Chown's magnificent 7mm scale Irish layout, which has several stations and uses correct bell codes and block instruments to communicate between them. At exhibitions it creates a sense of team spirit and purpose between operators and avoids that awful moment when the man on the controller shouts to the man in the fiddle yard "Let's have a goods train next!"

It is also educational: by operating correctly and displaying the timetable in some way to the viewing public, you can help educate a new generation of enthusiasts about how steam railways used to work.

What elements are needed for authentic operation? I believe they are:

- An analysis of traffic requirements
- Realistic trackplans
- Working signals, bells and block instruments
- The use of working timetables
- Rules and regulations
- Correct train formations
- Realistic movement

I will be examining each of these elements in the following chapters.

In addition, there is a difference between the authentic operation of a model railway at home and one at exhibitions. At home you can do things the way the prototype did and have fun shunting your stopping goods train for an hour or so if you wish. However, at an exhibition we need to keep the public entertained and some compromises are necessary. I discuss these in the final chapter.

LBSCR E4 0-6-2T No. 468 Midhurst shunts the goods yard at Plumpton Green. The rest of its train is in the Down platform while there is a passenger train in the Up platform.   BARRY LUCK

NER Class P 0-6-0 No. 1822 runs into Calder Bridge Goods Yard with a local goods service.   BARRY NORMAN

CHAPTER ONE
ANALYSING TRAFFIC REQUIREMENTS

What did the real railway do?
Before deciding what facilities (platforms, sidings, engine sheds, etc.) to provide at any new location, the railway companies would have had to estimate the likely nature and volume of traffic that it would have to handle. They might get this wrong and provide insufficient facilities, in which case extra platforms or sidings would have to be built. Alternatively, they might overestimate the likely traffic and provide more platforms, sidings, etc. than were actually needed.

As time went on, railway traffic generally grew throughout the 19th and early 20th century, so the railways expanded their facilities to enable them to cope with the additional trains. Single lines were doubled, double lines were quadrupled, additional goods lines were provided and new sorting sidings built. As we all know, this process was sadly reversed after traffic volumes declined in the late 1950s, leading to the notorious Beeching cuts in the 1960s.

Railways were dynamic and changed according to circumstances, so modellers need to think about what their location would be like in their chosen period. However, the main thing driving change, both for expansion and contraction, was the need to handle the traffic on the line.

How can we replicate this in model form?
In order to understand what the traffic requirements for your chosen location would be, you need to do a bit of research. If you are modelling a real

An unidentified L&YR Aspinall 4-4-2 leaving York with a train of bogie stock in Pre-Grouping days. The original station at York was a terminus inside the city walls; consequently trains heading through the city had to reverse. To avoid this, a magnificent new through station was opened in 1877.
LYRS COLLECTION

This wonderful photograph shows an L&YR Barton Wright 4-4-0 heading an express passenger train past Pendlebury, near Salford, in Pre-Grouping days. The L&YR's original route from Liverpool to Manchester via Bolton became extremely congested and so the company built a new, shorter route via Atherton.
LYRS COLLECTION

L&YR Aspinall 0-6-0 No. 1028 shunts the wagons from an incoming goods train into the yard at Eccleston.

SIMON EDMUNDS

L&YR Barton Wright 0-6-0 No. 952, t
Goods loco, shunts the coal sidings at Ec
SIMON EDM

location you should try and obtain a copy of the Working Timetable (WTT) for the line in your chosen period. Working Timetables are documents which give railway operators details of all the trains scheduled to run on a given section of line, including passenger, goods and mineral workings, plus light engines, trip workings, etc.

Obtaining a copy of the relevant WTT will give you details of all the train services on the line at that time. The appendix to the WTT may also give valuable information about your location, such as particular operating restrictions or arrangements. For example, it may say that a certain number of wagons can be

An L&NWR train is signalled into the Goods Loop at Calderwood with a fitted freight. The L&NWR had running powers over this section of the L&YR's Calder Valley main line.   AUTHOR

NER Tennant 2-4-0 No. 274 passes Lowburn Park with an Express Passenger train from Newcastle to Carlisle. On the right one of the Tyneside electric locos stands with a brake van.   STEVE FLINT, CTY. RAILWAY MODELLER

propelled from a set of sorting sidings to a private siding or run without a brake van. Suggestions for how to get hold of the relevant documents can be found in Chapter 4.

If you are modelling an imaginary location, you need to put it into context by creating a history of the line and a justification for its construction and development. For example, if you are modelling a line in the Welsh Valleys, the justification for the construction of the railway would most likely be the movement of coal from pit to port.

Alternatively, if you are modelling a city terminus, the justification would be the need to get large numbers of people to and from work every day. In my case, Eccleston had two cotton mills and was surrounded by rich arable farming, so there are two sources of goods traffic. Passenger traffic would be local in nature, such as people going into Preston for the market or shopping, with excursion traffic to the Lancashire coast in summer. Armed with this information, I examined several WTTs for similar L&YR branch line termini and decided that I could handle the traffic on offer with a regular passenger service to Preston; a daily return service to Blackburn; and two goods services – one a Through Goods working from Lostock Hall conveying traffic from all over the L&YR system and beyond, and the other a Pilot Goods working from Croston Sidings conveying traffic from the Liverpool direction.

From the background story that you create about your chosen location you can then decide what sort of traffic would be seen there and from that you can determine the sort of trackplan and signalling you will need.

This wonderfully atmospheric shot of Chris Pendlenton's North Shields is full of operational interest. On the left the yard pilot waits with a train of tank wagons while a train of loaded minerals departs from Collingwood Yard and a train of empties arrives.

CHRIS PENDLENTON

CHAPTER TWO
DEVISING REALISTIC TRACKPLANS

The terminus at Holmfirth in 1955 showing the station building, platform, canopy and goods shed.

What did the real railway do?

Real railways designed their trackplans to deal with the traffic they anticipated handling. If and when that traffic changed, they modified their trackplans accordingly. As profit-maximising companies, they sought the most economical solutions and were not keen to install trackwork which was not likely to be used. Having said that, even the most casual study of pre-Grouping trackplans reveals a much greater complexity than will be seen on today's railway. Double and single slips, three-way points and multiple crossovers abounded at busy junctions and terminal stations. Even some relatively modest passing stations seem to have had a lot of trackwork to deal with limited train movements. The explanation for this apparent contra-diction lies in the signalling systems in use at different periods of time. Traditional mechanical block signalling required long headways between trains for safety reasons. Complex trackwork was required at busy junctions and terminal stations to allow parallel moves and deal with the huge volume of traffic, often moving at relatively slow speeds in such areas. Today's simplified trackplans can deal with high volumes of traffic due to the use of multiple aspect signalling and higher train speeds.

Some railway companies had distinctive house styles when it came to trackplans. The most notable of these was the Midland Railway whose dislike of facing points led to it designing trackplans which avoided these at all possible locations, except junctions and the approaches to terminal stations. My favourite pre-Grouping railway company, the Lancashire and Yorkshire, had a distinctive design for its double-track branch line termini which I illustrate in the next section. On the other hand, the North Eastern Railway had a very individualistic style of track layouts which may be explained by the fact that one of its constituents was the Stockton and Darlington – usually thought of as the world's first proper railway.

Having an authentic trackplan ensures not only that your layout looks like the prototype, but also that it works realistically and that the signals are positioned correctly.

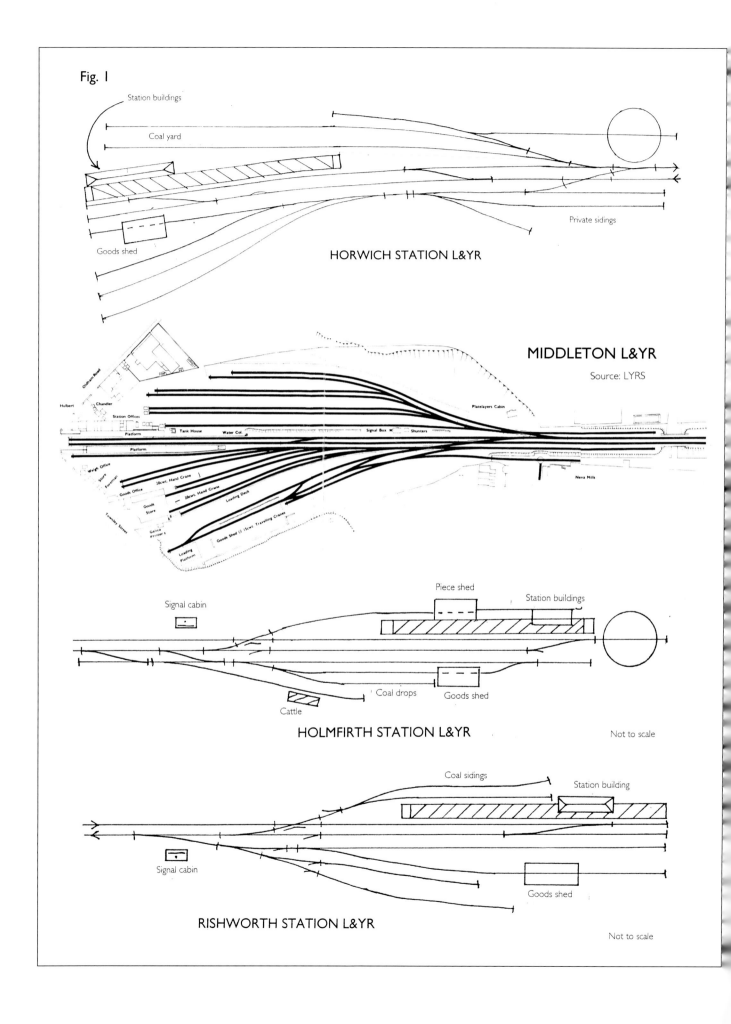

Fig. 1

Station buildings

Coal yard

Goods shed

HORWICH STATION L&YR

Private sidings

MIDDLETON L&YR

Source: LYRS

Oldham Road
Hulbert
Chandler
Station Offices
Platform
Tank House   Water Col
Platform
Weigh Office
Store
Foreman
Goods Office   18cwt. Hand Crane
Goods
Store   30cwt. Hand Crane   Loading Deck
Townley Street
Calico
Printers
Loading
Platform   Goods Shed (2 15cwt. Travelling Cranes)

Platelayers Cabin
Signal Box   Shunters
Neva Mills

Piece shed

Signal cabin   Station buildings

Coal drops   Goods shed

Cattle

HOLMFIRTH STATION L&YR

Not to scale

Coal sidings   Station building

Signal cabin   Goods shed

RISHWORTH STATION L&YR

Not to scale

How can we replicate this in model form?

The main thing to do if you want to design a realistic trackplan which will provide you with interesting operation is to study what your chosen railway company did. Whether you model the pre-Grouping, Grouping or British Railways era, there are plenty of books of trackplans available covering everything from the smallest branch line termini to major junctions, goods yards, loco sheds and the largest city stations (see Bibliography). Line societies and OS maps are other useful sources of information and so are the archives at the National Railway Museum or the National Archive at Kew.

Of course, the safest way to ensure that your track plan is realistic is to make a model of a real location. That way no-one can argue that you got it wrong! Many modellers do this with impressive results. (Incidentally, there is an added attraction of modelling a real location; I have modelled an imaginary location and have spent hours trying to work out what the L&YR would have done if they had built a branch line to Eccleston. What design of station building would they have used? Would the walls be brick or stone? What sort of signals would they have used and where would they be located? If you model a real location, all these questions are answered for you!)

However, real railway locations were often large and sprawling and the only way to model them is to go in for selective compression, perhaps shortening the length of platforms and loops or reducing the number of sidings. Some modellers are happy to accept such compromises but others are not and many therefore choose to model 'might have been' imaginary locations. The most common way of doing this is to choose a location which did not have a railway and imagine that it did. You then have the challenge of working out what your chosen railway company would have done in your imaginary circumstances. I adopted this approach when I planned my L&YR branch terminus 'Eccleston'. Eccleston is a real village in West Lancashire which never had a railway. I imagined that the L&YR was persuaded to build a branch line to Eccleston from Croston on the Preston to Liverpool main line. So if that had happened, what would

This is unfortunately a poor quality photograph, but it perfectly illustrates the track layout at Rishworth with the coal sidings on the left, the platform and loop in the centre and the goods yard on the right.

LYRS COLLECTION

An Aspinall 2-4-2T, pictured in LMS days, in the carriage siding at Horwich with empty stock waiting to work one of the passenger trains run in connection with the end of the working day at Horwich Loco Works.

LYRS COLLECTION

the trackplan look like? To decide this, I got hold of the trackplans of several L&YR branch termini. These were obtained from the L&YR Society's series of branch line booklets and also from the society's collection of Ordnance Survey maps. I am sure other line societies would have similar information available.

Here at *Fig. 1* are four examples which influenced my final design: Horwich and Middleton from Lancashire, Holmfirth and Rishworth from Yorkshire. It seems to me that these plans have some similarities: firstly, they are all double track. The L&YR did have some single-track branch lines, such as

Holcombe Brook and Clayton West, but most of the company's branch lines were double-track in order to cope with the considerable volume of traffic they handled. This, of course, is one of the attractions of modelling the L&YR: it was an extremely busy railway with lots of operational potential! In three of the four cases illustrated there is only one platform face with a run-round loop formed of two trailing crossovers. In all cases the goods yards were extensive and spread on both sides of the station. Horwich also had a couple of private sidings running in the opposite direction to the goods yard off the headshunt and I thought this was a

An Aspinall 2-4-2T waiting in the departure platform at Middleton, an urban branch line in north Manchester. Note the goods yard on the left and the coal yard on the right.   LYRS COLLECTION

feature which would add operational interest. The resulting trackplan for Eccleston is shown at *Fig. 2*.

For 'Calder Bridge' we adopted a similar approach. We were looking for a trackplan which would be distinctively North Eastern in origin, but which could be adapted to suit our requirements. After looking at a number of NER trackplans, we eventually settled on the branch terminus at Alston which is shown at *Fig. 3*. Alston was a single-track terminus in rural Cumbria, whereas Calder Bridge, which was supposed to be near Wakefield in West Yorkshire, needed to have a double-track layout to cope with heavier volumes of traffic.

ECCLESTON STATION L&YR

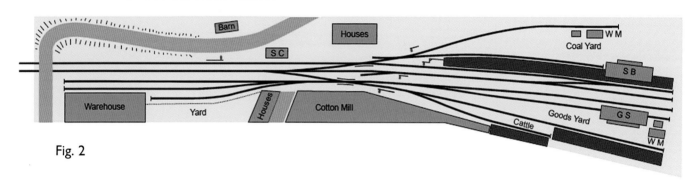

Fig. 2

The trackwork forming the station throat at Eccleston which was based on typical L&YR practice.
SIMON EDMUNDS

The trackplan for Calder Bridge is at *Fig. 4* and a comparison with *Fig. 3* will show how we used the key elements of Alston – the trainshed over the main platform, the carriage siding inside the trainshed, the turntable at the end of the platform giving access to the engine shed and the run-round loop – to form the basis for our layout. We added double track, the characteristic NER coal drops and turned the goods yard round to fit the space we had available.

I hope these two examples give you some ideas of how it is possible to adapt trackplans from your favourite railway company in designing your own layout.

Some trackplans were common all over the country and an example of this is the double-track through station layout at Bakewell on the Midland Railway's magnificent route through the Peak

The end of the train shed at Alston showing the engine shed on the left (through which you can see the signal box), the carriage siding, the platform with ex-LNER J39 No. 64858 having arrived with a passenger train and, on the right, the station building.   O. H. PROSSER

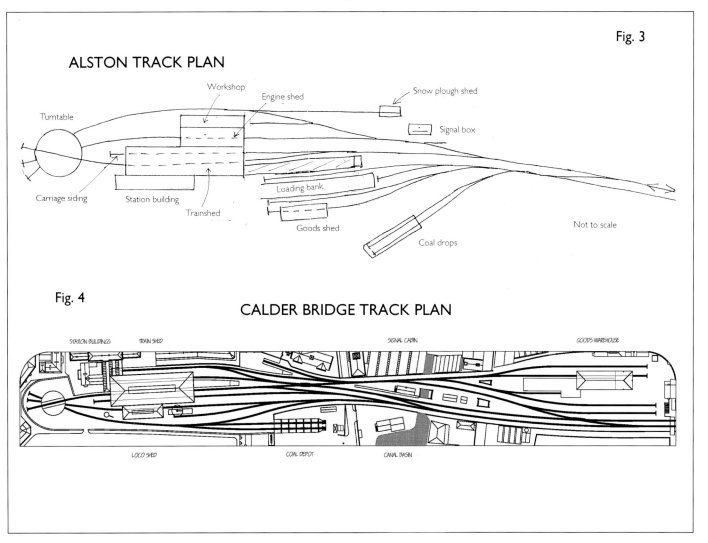

Fig. 3

ALSTON TRACK PLAN

Turntable · Carriage siding · Station building · Trainshed · Workshop · Engine shed · Loading bank · Goods shed · Coal drops · Snow plough shed · Signal box · Not to scale

Fig. 4

CALDER BRIDGE TRACK PLAN

STATION BUILDINGS · TRAIN SHED · SIGNAL CABIN · GOODS WAREHOUSE · LOCO SHED · COAL DEPOT · CANAL BASIN

District shown in *Fig. 5*. Trailing access to the goods yard is provided from both running lines meaning goods trains could easily drop off and collect wagons. A single slip provides a connection between the up and down lines and also means a loco could run-round a raft of wagons placed in the loop line.

Examples of this sort of trackplan could be found on many other railway systems,

Right: The north end of Bakewell station in July 1957 showing the very typical Midland Railway track layout.
STAN ROBERTS COLLECTION / PEAK RAIL

BAKEWELL TRACK PLAN

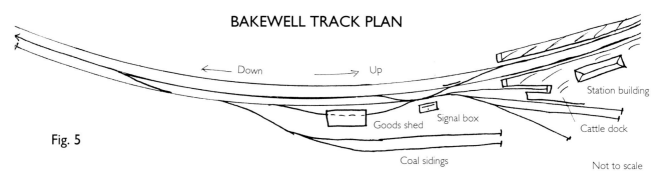

Fig. 5

Down ← → Up

Goods shed

Signal box

Station building

Cattle dock

Coal sidings

Not to scale

The complex train formation at the entrance to Southport Chapel Street station which was the terminus of lines approaching from three directions: Liverpool, Wigan and Preston.
LYRS COLLECTION

CHAPTER THREE
USING WORKING SIGNALS

This fascinating array of signals was at Blackpool Talbot Road (now Blackpool North) in L&YR days. The excursion platforms are seen on the right and the goods shed on the left.
LYRS COLLECTION

What did the real railway do?
From the very earliest days of rail transport, the railway companies were conscious of the need to maintain safety and control the traffic. Early railways developed primitive signalling systems using flags and bar or disc signals. As the 19th Century progressed and the network spread, more complex signalling systems were developed, leading eventually to the universal adoption of the Absolute Block Signalling Regulations, enforced by the Board of Trade.

Under this system the basic principle was established that the track was divided into block sections and station limits and that only one train was permitted in each block section at any one time. The block section was controlled by a signal box, or block post, and the signalman in charge was responsible for ensuring that only one train was in the block section. He did this by exchanging bell codes with the signalboxes 'in rear' (i.e. back in the direction of travel) and 'in advance' (i.e. forward in the direction of travel). These bell codes were reinforced by the movement of needles on block instruments, so the signalmen had both an audible and a visual reminder of the state of the block section.

Obviously this system was still subject to human error: a signalman could forget that he had admitted a train to a block section and then admit another one, so further safety devices, such as electrical locks and track circuits, were built into the system as time went by. In busy areas, such as the approach to terminal stations and on busy goods lines, variations were allowed to admit more than one train into a block section at low speeds and under strictly controlled conditions. This was known as permissive block working.

The Absolute Block System applied to double-track (and multiple-track) lines, but of course there were many hundreds of miles of single-track lines on the network and these needed special regulations to ensure that only one train – travelling in either direction – was admitted to the block section at any one time. These involved a system of working where a train could not enter a block section unless the driver was in possession of a token or train staff. Electrical systems were devised which linked the token instruments in adjacent signalboxes to enable successive tokens to be withdrawn, allowing trains to proceed one after another, rather than alternating.

This is a complex yet fascinating subject which has been explained in great

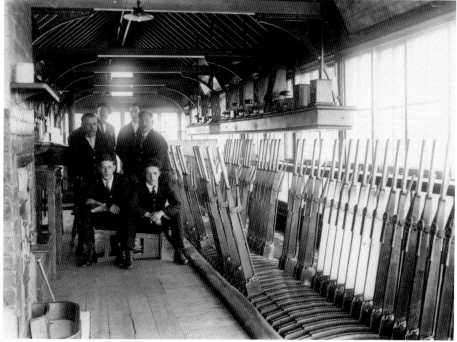

The interior of Kirkham North Junction signal box in Pre-Grouping days. This was a very large box with 95 levers built by the L&YR in 1903 to handle the busy junctions of two lines to Blackpool Central (via the coast and direct) and the line to Blackpool Talbot Road and Fleetwood. It would probably have been worked by two signalmen and a lad whose job was to record everything in the train register.
LYRS COLLECTION

A typical L&YR ground signal at an unknown location .
R. S. CARPENTER COLLECTION

Left: These lovely ex-Midland Railway signals can be found at Embsay on the Embsay and Bolton Abbey Steam Railway. This picture shows one of the shunting signals in the off position authorising a move into the engine shed.   AUTHOR

detail in numerous signalling books. Several are listed in the bibliography, but if you want a quick and easy introduction, I recommend the Ian Allan ABC book *Signalling in the Age of Steam* by Michael Vanns.

How can we replicate this in model form?
Signalling is so fundamental to the way that real railways operated that it is an essential component of almost all model railways. Yet many modellers consider it last, if at all, after they have completed all the track, buildings and scenery! I have lost count of the number of layouts I have seen at model railway exhibitions which either have no signals or have ones which do not work.

This is not only sad, it is a shame because operating a model railway which has correct and working signals is a lot more satisfying than operating one which does not. For example, my own layout has a fully-interlocked mechanical lever frame which means it is not possible to pull off the signals unless the points are set correctly. This not only eliminates operator error, but also makes working the layout feel much more authentic than it did before the lever frame was installed.

So my fundamental recommendation is to build signals and their operating mechanisms into the layout from the beginning, not as an afterthought. Indeed the signals should be considered an integral part of the track-planning process. On 'Eccleston', the sequence of construction was baseboards, track, electrics, signalling. Only after all that was installed and working properly did I start work on buildings and scenery. Installing the signals first also has the advantage that you do not damage buildings or scenery while doing so.

Having working signals also helps at exhibitions where the viewing public can anticipate movements when a signal is raised or lowered; this helps to maintain their interest even when nothing is actually moving.

Authentic model signals also help to give your layout identity; each railway company had its own signalling style and these were as distinctive as its architecture or locomotives. Nothing says GWR more than its characteristic lower quadrant signals and some of these can still be seen

Apprentices from Horwich Works built a Gauge 1 layout to teach the principles of signalling to L&YR trainee signalmen. It can now be seen at the National Railway Museum in York where it is demonstrated regularly.
AUTHOR

An ex-L&NWR ground frame at Chwilog, on the line between Caernarvon and Afon Wen, photographed in the late 1950s.

R. S. CARPENTER COLLECTION

Traditional mechanical signalling is rapidly disappearing from Network Rail but can still be seen on preserved railways. This is the superb signal gantry at Bury Bolton Street on the East Lancashire Railway.   AUTHOR

Ex-L&YR 2-4-2T No. 50650 approaching the terminus at Holcombe Brook with a motor train from Bury Bolton Street on the last day of passenger services in 1952.

R. S. CARPENTER COLLECTION

in use today at locations such as Worcester and Shrewsbury.

Making signals is not particularly difficult and kits are available from Model Signal Engineering (*www.modelsignals. com*).

Designing the signalling system you need for your layout involves more enjoyable research. If you are modelling a real location, you have a distinct advantage: photographs will show the type and location of the signals used during your chosen period and you may also be able to track down signalbox diagrams from the appropriate line society or the Signalling Record Society.

If, like me, you are modelling a fictitious location, you will have to research the typical type and location of signals at similar locations on your chosen

Aspinall 2-4-2T No. 724 hauls its passenger train away from Eccleston under the bracketed starting signal.
SIMON EDMUNDS

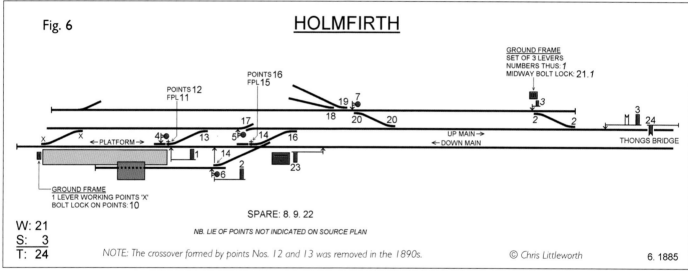

Fig. 6

HOLMFIRTH

© Chris Littleworth

6. 1885

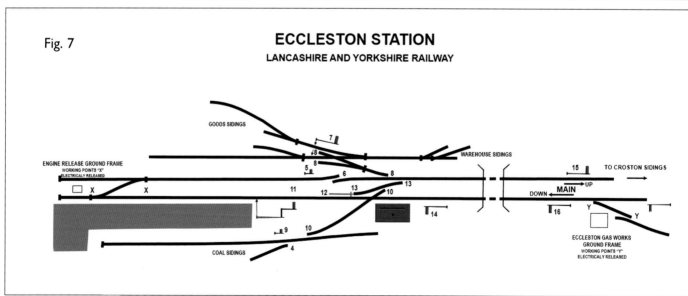

Fig. 7

ECCLESTON STATION
LANCASHIRE AND YORKSHIRE RAILWAY

railway. There are various books of trackplans and signalling available and these may be able to help you, or you could once again approach the appropriate line society or the Signalling Record Society.

When I was planning the signalling for 'Eccleston' I looked at the trackplans discussed in Chapter 1 and worked out the type and location of signals used using photographs in books or obtained from the L&YR Society. As with the trackplans, some common themes emerged: there was a home and starting signal to control arrivals and departures, there were ground or subsidiary signals to control movements out of the goods sidings or run-round loop onto the main passenger running lines, but there were no signals to control movements in the opposite direction. Presumably the L&YR felt they were not necessary at small stations where all moves were visible to the signalman who could authorise drivers to proceed by use of hand signals or lamps. The signalling diagram for Holmfirth is at *Fig. 6* and shows some of these principles.

Naturally enough, the signalling diagram I designed for 'Eccleston' (see *Fig. 7*) followed these principles. I made the signals from parts supplied by Model Signal Engineering and found doing so very satisfying. Installing them on the layout immediately started to give the layout L&YR character.

Making the signals work was a challenging but satisfying exercise: I decided to use exclusively mechanical methods, as the real railway would have done in such a location. The signals are therefore worked by a much-modified MSE lever frame and the GEM Mercontrol wire-in-tube system.

On more complex layouts, other operating systems can be used. My friend Barry Luck has a mechanically-interlocked lever frame on his layout 'Plumpton Green', but the levers work micro-switches which in turn control Tortoise point motors which are connected to the points and signals. Some modellers are now using servo motors developed for the model aircraft hobby which are cheaper and take up less space, but require an electronic control system.

Behind the scenes at Eccleston showing the lever frame, block instruments, bell and section switches.
SIMON EDMUNDS

Steve Hall with two of the full-size ex-BR block instruments on his layout Drighlington for Adwalton. Interestingly, they are of different orientation; the one on the left has the 'Line Clear' (green) indication on the left while the one on the right has the same indication on the right.
JAMES MOORHOUSE

One set of Tyer's two-position block instruments, scratchbuilt by Barry Luck for Plumpton Green. On the left the bell and bell-plunger, on the right the signal indicators, and two more plungers. One gives the 'line clear' indication to the box in rear (the red arm in the box in rear comes off, and the white arm replicates this), and one to reset both signals on receipt of 'train entering section'. There is no 'train on line' indication.
BARRY LUCK

Of course, signalling systems do not just consist of signals, points and levers. The complete system requires the communication elements of bells and block instruments. Unfortunately, no manufacturer seems willing to make these on a commercial basis. Years ago, Tri-ang produced some miniature block instruments, incorporating bells, but these are now collectors' items. So the only way to obtain them is to make them yourself. Bells are not too difficult to obtain: on 'Eccleston' I originally used to use a set of standard doorbells from a DIY supermarket with the chime disabled. I also replaced the push button with a long-handled micro-switch screwed to the body of the bell. This worked very well. However, I now have a set of miniature block instruments, including bells, which were professionally made for a friend, on permanent loan which has solved the problem. These are shown in the photo on page 23.

If you have the money and the space, you can use real block instruments bought from eBay or railwayana auctions. Steve Hall does this on his extensive layout 'Drighlington and Adwalton Junction'. See photo on page 23.

Operating a layout which is correctly signalled and where communication between operators uses bells and block instruments greatly adds to the pleasure of running the trains themselves.

LBSCR B4 No. 64 Norfolk gets the 'right away' from the tall up platform starter at Plumpton Green. The adjacent shunt ahead arm (ringed) gives access to the main line from the up bay as far as the advanced starter.

BARRY LUCK

There are two lever frames controlling the points and signals at Plumpton Green; one represents the signal box, the other the London-end ground frame and the two are mechanically interlocked. All four signals in each direction (distant, home, starter, advanced starter) are included in the signal box lever frame. Only three are on the layout, but all eight are shown in the fiddle yards to control trains on and off the layout. The third lever frame (not interlocked) operates the goods yard points.

TIM VENTON

CHAPTER FOUR
DEVELOPING A WORKING TIMETABLE

What did the real railway do?

Real railway operation was not random: it was carefully planned. It had to be if it was to provide a good service to its passenger and freight customers and also to avoid getting itself into a terrible tangle, with locomotives, carriages and wagons all in the wrong places at the wrong times. Armies of clerks were employed to draw up complex timetables, rosters and schedules to ensure not only that the trains were in the right place at the right time, but that the appropriate staff were available to drive the trains, operate the signalboxes, staff the stations and goods depots, etc.

Not only did the railway companies issue public timetables, but they also produced much more complex working

timetables showing the timings of all trains in their appropriate categories, from express passenger services to the local goods trains. These were backed up by appendices listing the locations of water cranes and signalboxes, the gradients on each route, special operating requirements, etc. And if all this was not enough, weekly traffic notices were issued to all the operating staff showing any special trains, excursions or other variations to the routine.

No two days on the railway were ever the same, except perhaps for the most rural branch lines where the regular comings and goings of the local services were less liable to change. In more complex areas, however, trains ran late for a variety of reasons, extra trains had to be

run to cope with unexpected volumes of traffic and variations would occur thanks to seasonal or traffic requirements.

For example, trains would be provided to move fruit from the Vale of Evesham at harvest time, but these would not be run at other times of the year. On the passenger side of things, huge numbers of excursion trains were run to seaside resorts in the summer months, but not in winter.

Overseeing all this were the Control Offices who would manage the railway on an hour-by-hour basis. If one train was running late, another might be given its path in the timetable to keep the traffic moving. If a goods yard reported that it had more wagons to move than the planned train could take, a locomotive,

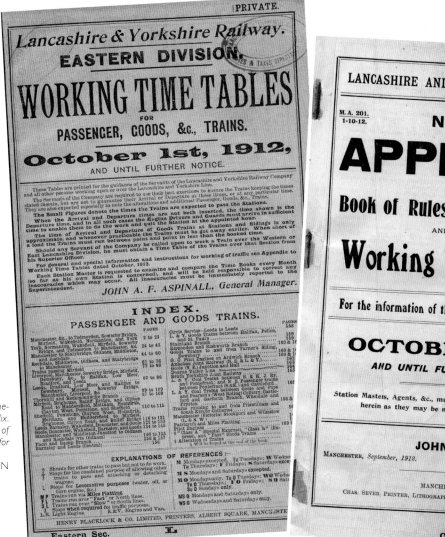

A typical Working Timetable and an appendix. These documents are full of useful information for modellers.
LYRS COLLECTION

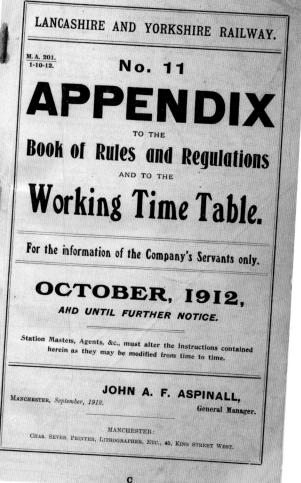

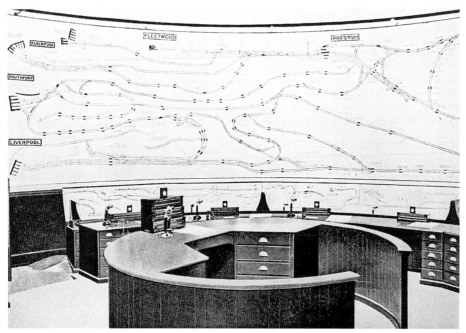

A section of the circular control office at Manchester Victoria which was established by the L&YR in 1915. In the centre is the Chief Controller's desk and behind is part of the Control Map showing the routes to Liverpool, Southport, Blackpool and Fleetwood.

LYRS COLLECTION

brake van and crew would be found to run a special or extra train. At a more local level, traffic was regulated by the signalmen working junctions or busy stations who often had to decide which trains to accept and which to hold at signals while paths or platforms became available. So although the lineside observer might have seen an apparently random series of trains passing his chosen location, it was in reality all carefully planned and managed.

How can we replicate this in model form?
Just as the movement of traffic on the real railway was carefully planned, so we should plan the activity on our model railway layouts. This is not a chore, but a satisfying exercise in its own right. It also prevents operators getting into a mess with too many locomotives in the fiddle yard and not enough on the layout.

The essential planning tool is the Working Timetable (WTT) which shows

An Aspinall 0-6-0 heading an ordinary passenger train formed of bogie stock past James Kenworthy's wagon works at Lockwood, near Huddersfield. On the right is the tender of an L&YR 0-8-0 and a 'Tin Tab' brake van with a reporting number in large numerals. These numbers were used by the Control Offices to monitor the movement of brake vans. Also of note are the tall junction signal and the fascinating collection of wagons in the background.

LYRS COLLECTION

the movement of all trains. How do you devise a WTT? Well, the real railway used pencils, rulers and graph paper to plot the movement of trains, avoid clashes and allocate 'paths' to different classes of train. Today they use computers to do the same sort of thing. For authenticity's sake, modellers could do the same and if you have a large layout featuring several stations, goods yards, locomotive depots, etc, you may well find it useful. However, for those modellers who build a branch terminus or other single railway location, the arrival/departure sequence is probably sufficient.

The first thing to do is to obtain a WTT for the location you are modelling, if it is a real one, or for the general area if it is an imaginary location. They can be obtained from a number of sources. Firstly, the relevant line society for your favourite location will probably have a selection covering different historical periods. Secondly, WTTs can often be obtained from model railway exhibitions

or these days from eBay. Failing that, you will have to do your own research by going to the National Archives at Kew or the National Railway Museum at York.

If you are modelling a real location you can go through the WTT and identify the types, frequency and timings of trains to be seen there. You may wish to follow the WTT as closely as possible or you may wish to simply devise your own sequence based on a representative range of trains which worked the line in question. Some busy mainline locations had services which ran from far away passing through and to replicate the full WTT would require an enormous range of locos and stock. A representative selection might be more achievable.

If you are modelling a fictional location, you need to develop a convincing history of the line and how it linked into the real railway. For example, you might be modelling a station on an imaginary branch line which connected with the mainline at a particular junction.

If you obtain a WTT for the line that the junction is on, you can work out which trains would have stopped there and then how your branchline trains could connect with them.

Real WTTs give timings for trains at key points such as junctions and at stations and goods yards, whether they are passing through a section of line or calling. You can incorporate timings into your own WTT if you wish – indeed some modellers run their layouts to speeded-up clocks – but this is not necessary and a simple sequence of trains is sufficient, especially for exhibition operation.

When it came to devising a sequence for my own layout 'Eccleston', I got hold of a number of WTTs for L&YR branch lines from the L&YR Society. These indicated the sort of traffic these branches carried. The L&YR's WTT for the Holmfirth branch in 1896 is at *Fig. 8*. As you can see, the types of trains to be seen on the branch included ordinary

---

Extract from Holmfirth Branch Working Timetable 1896   Fig. 8

Up trains

Type of train	Pass	Pass	Exp. G	Pass	Pass	Pass	Pass	Pass	G&C	Pass	Pass	Pass	Pass	Exp.G	Pass	G&C
From	Mir	Bfd	A	Mir	Hudd	Hudd	Hudd	Halifax	Lock	Halifax	Hudd	Halifax	Hudd	S.Br.	Hudd	H.Jt.
Huddersfield	5.07	6.03	6.00	7.05	7.25	8.50	9.43	10.27	-	12/05	12/50	1/25	2/30	3/04	4/05	4/25
Brockholes Junction	5.22	6.18	6.25	7.20	8.05	9.05	9.58	10.52	10.38	12/20	1/07	1/40	2/45	3/19	4/20	4/40
Thongs Bridge	5.26	6.22	6.45	7.24	8.09	9.09	10.02	10.56	11.15	12/24	1/11	1/44	2/49	3/23	4/24	4/45
Holmfirth	5.30	6.26	6.55	7.28	8.15	9.15	10.06	11.02	11.20	12/28	1/15	1/48	2/53	3/27	4/28	5/00

Down trains

Type of train	Pass	Pass	Goods	Pass	Goods	Pass	Pass	Pass	Pass	Pass	Pass	Goods	Goods	Pass	Pass	Pass
Holmfirth	5.45	6.40	7.20	7.37	8.20	8.30	9.30	9.57	11.00	12/07	12/40	12/45	1/20	1/50	2/00	3/07
Thongs Bridge	5.48	6.43	-	7.40	-	8.33	9.33	10.00	11.03	12/10	12/43	1/00	1/40	1/54	2/03	3/10
Brockholes	5.52	6.47	7.35	7.44	8.35	8.37	9.37	10.04	11.07	12/14	12/47	1/27	2/02	1/58	2/07	3/14
Huddersfield	6.09	7.03	-	8.00	-	8.53	9.53	10.20	11.23	12/30	1/03	2/12	2/28	2/17	2/23	3/30
To	Bfd		Mir	Bfd	Mir	Bfd	Bkp	Halifax	S.Br.	Hfx	Hfx	Mir	Mir	S.Br.*	**	Bfd
					MO							SX	SO	SO		

Pass	Ordinary passenger train	A	Aintree Sorting Sidings	Bkp?	??	
Exp. G	Express Goods	Hudd	Huddersfield	*	Through Carriage to Blackpool Central	
G&C	Goods and cattle	Lock	Lockwood	**	On Saturdays takes Transit Van to Lockwood	
Mir	Mirfield	S.Br.	Sowerby Bridge			
Bfd	Bradford	H.Jt.	Hillhouse Junction			

The terminus at Holmfirth in LYR days with a saddle tank in the loop. The station buildings are seen on the right and the goods shed on the left.   LYRS COLLECTION

Fig. 9

Holmfirth movement sheet

Time	Arrival	Departure
5.30	Passenger from Mirfield	
5.45		Passenger to Mirfield
6.26	Passenger from Bradford	
6.40		Passenger to Huddersfield
6.55	Express Goods from Aintree Sorting Sidings	
7.20		Goods to Mirfield
7.28	Passenger from Mirfield	
7.37		Passenger to Bradford
8.15	Passenger from Huddersfield	
8.20		Goods to Mirfield Mondays only
8.30		Passenger to Bradford
9.15	Passenger from Huddersfield	
9.30		Passenger to Bkp (?)
9.57		Passenger to Halifax
10.06	Passenger from Huddersfield	
11.00		Passenger to Sowerby Bridge
11.02	Passenger from Halifax	
11.20	Goods and cattle from Lockwood	
12/07		Passenger to Halifax
12/28	Passenger from Halifax	
12/40		Passenger to Halifax
12/45		Goods to Mirfield Except Saturdays
1/15	Passenger from Huddersfield	
1/20		Goods to Mirfield Saturdays only
1/48	Passenger from Halifax	
1/50		Passenger to Sowerby Bridge Saturdays only: Through Carriage to Blackpool Central
2/00		Passenger to Huddersfield
2/53	Passenger from Huddersfield	
3/07		Passenger to Bradford
3.27	Express Goods from Sowerby Bridge	
4/50		Passenger to Halifax
5/00	Goods and Cattle from Hillhouse Junction	

passenger, express goods, goods and cattle and ordinary goods. There was a frequent service of passenger trains to a wide variety of destinations and even a through carriage to Blackpool on Saturdays. I am afraid I do not know where 'Bkp' is: possible it is Blackpool but it would seem unlikely that there would be a train across the Pennines from Holmfirth to Blackpool on weekdays.

Incidentally, one of the attractions of modelling the L&YR is the sheer busyness of the system; this was not a railway serving rural England, but rather the industrial heartlands and as such it carried huge volumes of traffic, both passenger and goods. That is why most of its branch lines were double track.

From the Holmfirth branch WTT I have compiled a movement sheet for the terminus at Holmfirth which is at *Fig. 9*. Unfortunately, this has shown up some workings which I cannot explain, such as the 9.57 passenger train to Halifax which appears from nowhere, i.e. there has not been an arrival to bring in a locomotive and carriages from which to form it. I can only surmise that there was an empty stock movement which has not been shown in the WTT. Perhaps empty stock and light engine movements were not shown in the L&YR's WTTs in 1896 as they were in later years. Similarly, the last train of the day is the arrival of a goods and cattle train. There was no engine shed at Holmfirth and so, after shunting its train, presumably the loco ran light engine to the nearest L&YR shed, Mirfield.

For 'Eccleston' I decided I would need four types of train: two local passenger services (one to Preston and one to Blackburn), a through goods working and a pilot goods (the L&YR term for a pick-up goods) working. I tried to imagine a typical day at Eccleston, starting with the early morning goods workings, then a regular flow of passenger working through the day interspersed with goods traffic, and then the evening goods workings to collect wagons for onward movement overnight.

Unfortunately, although the trackplan is authentic, it is also rather restrictive; there is no bay platform or carriage siding here, so when a passenger train arrives, all it can do is depart again! To enliven the routine operation of passenger traffic, I therefore added movements of non-passenger coaching stock such as fish vans, horse boxes, etc, and these are included in the sequence to ensure they start and finish in the same places. In real life the guard's van on passenger trains would be used to carry parcels, mail and news-papers. This traffic can be indicated by suitable stacks of parcels or trolleys on the platform.

The Eccleston operating sequence is at *Fig. 10*. At the time of writing I only have one passenger train, but I am able to borrow another set of carriages from my friend David Carter to enable me to run the Blackburn train. One day I will build the kits I have on the shelf so that I have a second passenger train of my own! If you read through the sequence, you will also note the arrival and departure of a North Eastern Railway Saloon and Carriage Truck. These are provided at exhibitions by another friend, John Thompson, and form a continuing link with the North East. The sequence is planned so that all

Fig. 10

Eccleston Working Timetable

Move	Fiddle Yard operator	Station operator
1. Through Goods from Lostock Hall to Eccleston. Conveys empty L&Y merchandise wagons and loaded minerals. Loco A	Offer Through Goods 1 to Eccleston. Prepare six-wheeled Passenger Train: loco, carriages, fish van.	Accept Through Goods. Drive Through Goods to home signal. Drive Through Goods to platform. R/R. Shunt BV to No. I Siding. Shunt loaded mineral wagons to coal yard. R/R merchandise wagons. Shunt merchandise wagons to warehouse sidings. Couple loco to BV in No. 1 Siding. Isolate loco.
2. Passenger Train from Preston to Eccleston. Six-wheeled carriages. Conveys fish van from Fleetwood. Loco B	Offer Passenger Train to Eccleston. Prepare Pilot Goods, including two cattle wagons.	Accept Passenger Train. Drive Passenger Train to platform. Set train back. R/R. Propel carriages along platform. Shunt fish van to No. 3 Siding. Couple loco to carriages in platform.
3. Passenger Train from Eccleston to Preston. Six-wheeled carriages. Loco B	Accept Passenger Train. Drive Passenger Train to FY.	Offer Passenger Train to Croston Sidings.
4. Pilot Goods from Croston Sidings to Eccleston. Conveys empty cattle wagons. Loco C	Offer Pilot Goods to Eccleston.	Accept Pilot Goods. Drive Pilot Goods to home signal. Drive Pilot Goods to station.
5. Light Engine and break van to Lostock Hall. Loco A	Accept LE&BV. Drive LE&BV to FY. Prepare Bogie Passenger Train.	Offer LE&BV to Croston Sidings. R/R Pilot Goods. Shunt BV to No. 1 Siding. Shunt wagons to goods yard. Move horsebox to another siding. Position cattle wagons for loading.
6. Passenger Train from Blackburn to Eccleston. Bogie carriages. Loco D	Offer Passenger Train to Eccleston. Drive Passenger Train to platform. Set train back. R/R. Propel carriages along platform. Collect horsebox from goods yard and couple to carriages in platform.	Make up outgoing Pilot Goods in No. 1 Siding.
7. Passenger Train from Eccleston to Blackburn. Bogie carriages. Conveys horsebox. Loco D	Accept Passenger Train. Drive Passenger Train to FY. Detach horsebox. Prepare Gas Works Trip.	Offer Passenger Train to Croston Sidings. Make up outgoing Pilot Goods in No. 1 Siding.
8. Trip working from Eccleston Gas Works to Eccleston station.	Propel Gas Works Trip to platform. Shunt coal sidings. Exchange wagons. Drive Gas Works Trip to FY. Prepare Through Goods 2.	Make up outgoing Pilot Goods in No. 1 Siding.
9. Through Goods from Lostock Hall to Eccleston. Loco A	Offer Through Goods 2 to Eccleston. Drive Through Goods to home signal. Drive Through Goods to platform.	Accept Through Goods. Make up outgoing Pilot Goods in No. 1 Siding.
10. Pilot Goods from Eccleston to Croston Sidings. Loco C	Accept Pilot Goods. Drive Pilot Goods to FY. Prepare Passenger Train: loco, carriages, North Eastern Saloon.	Offer Pilot Goods to Croston Sidings. R/R Through Goods. Shunt BV to end of No. I Siding. Shunt wagons to goods yard. Make up outgoing Through Goods in No. 1 Siding.
11. Passenger Train from Preston to Eccleston. Six-wheeled carriages. Conveys North Eastern Saloon. Loco B	Offer Passenger Train to Eccleston. Drive Passenger Train to platform. Set train back. R/R. Propel carriages along platform. Shunt North Eastern Saloon to spur. Couple to carriages in platform.	Accept Passenger Train. Shunt goods yard. Make up outgoing Through Goods in No. 1 Siding.
12. Passenger Train from Eccleston to Preston. Six-wheeled carriages. Loco B	Accept Passenger Train. Drive Passenger Train to FY. Prepare Bogie Passenger Train.	Offer Passenger Train to Croston Sidings. Shunt goods yard. Make up outgoing Through Goods in No. 1 Siding.
13. Passenger Train from Blackburn to Eccleston. Bogie carriages. Loco D	Offer Passenger Train to Eccleston. Drive Passenger Train from FY to Eccleston. Drive Passenger Train to platform. Set train back. R/R.	Accept Passenger Train. Shunt goods yard. Make up outgoing Through Goods in No. 1 Siding.
14. Through Goods from Eccleston to Lostock Hall. Loco A	Accept Through Goods. Drive Through Goods to FY.	Offer Through Goods to Croston Sidings. Shunt bogie carriages to No. 1 Siding.
15. Light Engine from Eccleston to Lostock Hall. Loco D	Accept Light Engine. Drive Light Engine from No. 1 Siding to FY. Prepare Pilot Goods.	Offer Light Engine to Croston Sidings.
16. Pilot Goods from Croston Sidings to Eccleston. Loco C	Offer Pilot Goods to Eccleston. Prepare six-wheeled passenger train: loco, six-wheeled carriages, horsebox.	Accept Pilot Goods. Drive Pilot Goods to home signal. Drive Pilot Goods to platform. R/R. Shunt BV to spur. Shunt yard.
17. Passenger Train from Preston to Eccleston. Six-wheeled carriages. Conveys horsebox. Loco B	Offer passenger train to Eccleston. Drive passenger train to Eccleston. R/R. Shunt horsebox to loading bank. Collect fish van. Couple to carriages in platform.	Accept passenger train. Shunt yard. Isolate goods loco and cattle wagons on headshunt.

19. Light Engine from Lostock Hall to Eccleston. Loco D	Offer Light Engine to Eccleston. Drive Light Engine to platform.	Accept Light Engine. Goods loco shunt yard. Make up outgoing Pilot Goods in loop, including cattle wagons. Isolate goods loco in headshunt. Couple passenger loco to carriages in No. 1 Siding. Shunt passenger train to platform.
20. Passenger train from Eccleston to Blackburn. Bogie carriages. Loco D	Accept Passenger Train. Drive Passenger Train to FY. Set up LE&BV.	Offer Passenger Train to Croston Sidings. Shunt yard. Make up outgoing Pilot Goods in loop, including cattle wagons.
21. Trip working from Eccleston Gas Works to Eccleston station.	Propel Gas Works Trip to platform. Shunt coal sidings. Exchange wagons. Drive Gas Works Trip to FY. Prepare Through Goods 2.	Shunt yard.
22. Light Engine and Break Van from Lostock Hall to Eccleston. Loco A	Offer LE&BV to Eccleston.	Accept LE&BV. Drive LE&BV to home signal. Drive LE&BV to platform.
23. Pilot Goods from Eccleston to Croston Sidings. Conveys cattle wagons. Loco C	Accept Pilot Goods. Drive Pilot Goods from loop to FY. Prepare Passenger Train: six-wheeled carriages	Offer Pilot Goods to Croston Sidings. R/R LE&BV. Shunt BV to No. 1 Siding. Collect empty minerals from coal sidings. Collect loaded merchandise wagons from warehouse sidings and R/R. Make up outgoing Through Goods in No 1 Siding.
24. Through Goods from Eccleston to Lostock Hall. Loco A	Accept Through Goods. Drive Through Goods to FY.	Offer Through Goods to Croston Sidings.
25. Passenger Train from Preston to Eccleston. Six-wheeled carriages. Loco B	Offer Passenger Train to Eccleston.	Accept Passenger Train. Drive Passenger Train to platform. Set train back. R/R. Collect North Eastern Saloon from spur. Couple to carriages in platform and propel train back along platform.
26. Passenger Train from Eccleston to Preston. Six-wheeled carriages. Conveys North Eastern Saloon. Loco B	Accept Passenger Train. Drive Passenger Train to FY. Detach North Eastern Saloon. Prepare Through Goods (Move No. 1)	Offer Passenger Train to Croston Sidings.

Eccleston start of sequence sheet   **February 2015**   **Fig. 11**

Fiddle yard

All locos

Through Goods 1: Five empty L&YR merchandise wagons, five loaded mineral wagons and brake van.

Through Goods 2: up to 10 wagons and brake van.

Passenger 1: Five six-wheeled carriages and fish van.

Passenger 2: Bogie carriages.

Pilot Goods: Two cattle wagons, up to eight other wagons and brake van.

NER Saloon and carriage truck.

Gas Works Trip: two empty mineral wagons and tar wagon.

Station

Horsebox at loading bank.

Three empty mineral wagons in coal sidings (plus ones that don't move).

Several general merchandise wagons in goods yard.

No. 1 Siding empty.

A couple of L&YR merchandise wagons in warehouse sidings.

---

the locomotives and rolling stock end up where they started from so that the whole thing can begin again. The Start of Sequence sheet is at *Fig. 11.* To help my fellow operators and any visitors, I also have a loco roster which is shown at *Fig. 12.*

Another way to work out a sequence is simply to make a list of all the trains that might appear at your location and then put them into a representative list. When I was planning the sequence for 'Calder Bridge', I began by making a list of all the trains we thought might have run into the station and then compared that with what locomotives and stock we had available to provide them. For example, we decided that we would need both NER and L&YR local passenger trains; my friend John Thompson could provide the NER example and I could provide the L&YR one. It was the same with the other categories of train we thought we needed, such as express passenger, local goods and mineral trains. I then identified all the possible locations where such trains could be on the layout: the main platform, the bay platform, the carriage siding, the goods yard and the fiddle yard.

Next I got a large sheet of paper and drew boxes on it to represent these five locations. Each train was represented by a piece of card the size of a business card; in fact I used some old business cards from work! I then drew up a representative sequence, based on a typical day's workings, and moved the cards around to ensure I avoided clashes. So, for example, when the L&YR passenger train arrived in the main platform, I moved the appropriate card from the fiddle yard box to the main platform box. The loco would then turn on the turntable at the end of the platform before running round its train. Then it shunted the train to the bay platform, so I moved the card to the bay platform box. All this time the

---

Fig. 12

Eccleston loco roster

Loco A:	Barton Wright 0-6-0 (No. 952)
Loco B:	Aspinall 2-4-2T (No. 724)
Loco C:	Aspinall 0-6-0ST (No. 753)
Loco D:	Aspinall 0-6-0 (No. 1028)
Loco E:	Aspinall 0-4-0ST ('Pug')

carriage siding was occupied by the stock for the NER express, so I knew I could not use that. I gradually worked through the day until, at the end of the sequence, all the stock was back where it started and we could begin the sequence all over again.

I subsequently did a separate exercise for locomotives to ensure we did not get a loco trapped at the back of the engine shed when it was needed to haul the next train! At the time I was doing this I had a busy job with a major UK company which involved regular travel from my home in Newcastle to London. I remember working out the locomotive moves on 'Calder Bridge' while travelling at 125 mph somewhere between Doncaster and King's Cross, much to the bemusement of my fellow passengers! An extract from the operating sequence for 'Calder Bridge' is at *Fig. 13*.

As you can see, this is fairly minimalist and may need some explanation; there are three operators who can drive trains, plus a fourth working the traverser. To explain the first couple of moves: the goods yard operator drives the NER goods from the traverser to the goods yard. When that move is completed the main panel operator drives the NER Passenger from Platform 1 to the traverser. When that train is safely out of the way, the station operator drives the NER goods loco from the goods yard to the turntable, turns it and stables it on the coal siding. Once the NER goods loco has left the goods yard, the goods yard operator can start shunting the yard using the pilot loco.

Operators were left to work out how to do these moves, including operating points and signals, by themselves. Communication between operators was purely verbal. I learned a lot from operating Calder Bridge in this way and it influenced my decision to write more detailed timetables in future and also to use block bells and instruments for communication.

As you devise your sequence, plan for a whole day's operation, so that you can include traffic that only ran at certain times of the day, such as commuter trains in the early morning and evening. Also try to keep to typical trains, like regular passenger and goods services; engineering trains or excursions are interesting to operate occasionally but were not seen that often in reality.

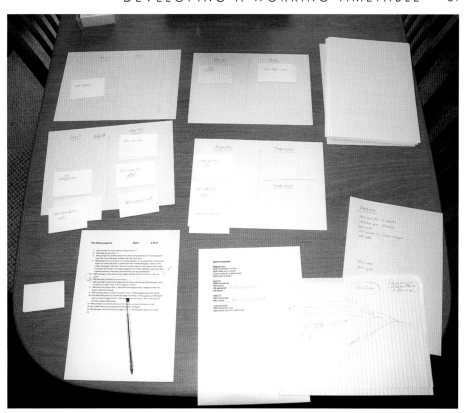

This photo shows how I compile a sequence timetable. Each A4 sheet of paper represents an origin or destination for a train; e.g. the fiddle yard, a station platform or a goods yard. Each small sheet of paper represents either a loco or a train. Having compiled a list of possible moves to start with, I move the small sheets of paper to the appropriate point on the A4 sheets and back again, writing it all down as I go along, and making sure everything ends up back where it started from. It is a simple system, but it works for me.   AUTHOR

Fig. 13

Calder Bridge operating sequence

Move	Goods Yard	Main panel	Station
1.	NER Goods from traverser to goods yard.		
2.	Shunt Yard.	NER Passenger 1 from Plat. 1 to traverser.	
			NER Goods loco from goods yard to turntable.
			Turn. Move to coal siding.
3.	Shunt Yard. Prepare coal cells shunt.		LYR Passenger from traverser to station.
			Turn train engine, then shunt stock to bay.
		Pilot to coal cells.	
4.	LE&BV from traverser to goods yard.		Coal cells shunt.
5.	Gas Works trip from traverser to goods yard.		Coal cells shunt.
6.	Shunt yard.	Gas Works loco to traverser.	Coal cells shunt.
7.	Shunt yard.	LYR Passenger from bay to traverser.	Coal cells shunt.
8.	LYR Minerals from goods yard to traverser.		
		Pilot to goods yard.	

DEVISING TIMETABLES FOR LAYOUTS by STEVE HALL

Before he retired, Steve Hall worked as a timetable planner for Network Rail and he has put his skills to use in devising timetables for his own and other people's layouts. Here he describes three different examples.

Every layout will be different and the requirements for the timetable or operating sequence will differ depending on the size and complexity of the layout and the method of operation employed. The following examples show how the timetable sequence can be displayed in different ways and be tailored to suit individual layouts depending on their size, complexity and number of operators.

Example 1 – Halifax King Cross

'Halifax King Cross' is a terminus to fiddle yard layout and is based on a British Railways (North Eastern region) 1960s what-might-have-been location based on the Halifax High Level Railway in the West Riding of Yorkshire. The layout is portable and designed to be exhibited at model railway shows requiring two operators, one operating the scenic section and the other in charge of the fiddle yard. The trackplan is at *Fig. 14.*

By 1960 the prototype timetable was freight only and consisted of just three trains per day (mostly coal traffic). For exhibition operation a more varied and intensive service is required and a little modellers licence has been applied.

The operating sequence consists of seventeen train movements and has been devised so that all the locos and rolling stock start and finish in the same place, so that the sequence can be repeated over and over without the need to reposition or handle any stock. It has evolved over the past twenty years while the layout has been on the exhibition circuit and the information contained within it should be sufficient for anyone to operate the layout with a minimum of instruction,

The operators drive the trains towards themselves so they can bring the trains to a halt in the right place and bell codes are used for communication between the two operators. The sequence instructions therefore include the appropriate bell codes for each train movement. The layout is operated by DCC control using a 4-digit address for each loco (last 4 digits of loco running number) and therefore the loco numbers are included in the sequence also.

The MS Word document consists of two pages. Page 1 has instructions for the terminus operator and includes details of all shunting movements (see *Fig. 15*) while page 2 is for the fiddle yard operator and details which traverser road should be used (see *Fig. 16*). The fiddle yard comprises a five-road traverser and each train is allocated to a specific road 1 to 5.

The sequence has been used at exhibitions for the past 15 years or so, although individual locomotives are changed for each exhibition. It is a simple matter to update the operating sequence by use of the CTRL+F function in MS Word to find and replace the loco number. It must be remembered, however, that if an alteration is made to

Steve Hall's Halifax King Cross is an excellent P4 layout which operates to a sequence timetable and uses block bells and instruments for communication between operators. It depicts the imagined terminus of the GNR/L&YR joint line from Holmfield in the 1960s. Here B1 4-6-0 No. 61161 departs with a parcels train while a WD Austerity 2-8-0 shunts the coal sidings.
CHRIS NEVARD / MODEL RAIL MAGAZINE

HALIFAX KING CROSS   Fig. 14

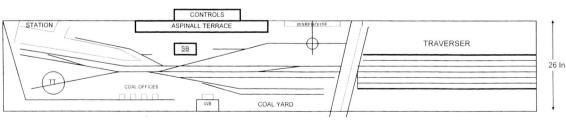

Fig. 15

HALIFAX KING CROSS OPERATOR INSTRUCTIONS

Move No.	Loco + Train formation / Shunting instructions	Bellcode
1	90310 + BV + 7 min + BV ARRIVES.	3
2	DMU (79007) DEPARTS 90310 Detach rear BV. Place 7 mins in coal yard. Couple BV's. on run round line. Run round BV's. attach + draw forward over No.1 crossover. Set back into main platform.	2 - 2 - 1
3	45208 + BV + 4 min + 3 vans + BV ARRIVES.	1 - 4
4	90310 + 2 BV's DEPARTS 45208 detach rear BV + 3 vans. Draw forward over No.5 X-over. Reverse into Warehouse siding and attach 3 vans. Place 3 vans in coal yard. Attach 3 vans from arrival road and place in warehouse siding. Place 4 mins in coal yard. Collect 3 vans + 2 mins from coal yard and couple to BV on arrival line. Run Round train.	1 - 1 - 3
5	82026 + Inspection Saloon ARRIVES AND DEPARTS via Up Line under Fiddle Yard control (takes place while 45208 performs shunt moves)	2 - 2 - 3
6	61161 + Empty Coaching Stock ARRIVES. (via UP line).	2 - 2 - 1
7	45208 + BV +3 vans + 2 min + BV DEPARTS 61161 shunts Stock to Bay platform.	1 - 4
8	68935 + Bogie Bolster + 3 Grampus + 2 Dogfish + Mermaid + BV ARRIVES	3
9	61161 DEPARTS LE 68935 reform train by swapping over Brake Van and Bogie Bolster wagon. Run Round Train.	2 - 3
10	45208 + 2 BV (Propelled) ARRIVES (at Stop board) Accept using 3 - 5 - 5	1 - 1 - 3
11	68935 + Bogie Bolster + Mermaid +2 Dogfish + 3 Grampus + BV DEPARTS 45208 run round BV's. Assemble train BV + 5 min + BV. Draw back to buffer stops.	3
12	90310 + 2 BV (hauled) ARRIVES Pause at stop board, detach BV's. Attach to train formed by 45208.	1 - 1 - 3
13	61161 LE ARRIVES (via UP line) in main platform	2 - 3
14	90310 + BV + 5 min + BV DEPARTS 61161 - shunt LE to Stock in Bay platform.	4 - 1
15	61161 + Empty Coaching Stock DEPARTS 45208 assemble train BV + 4 min + BV. + Run Round	2 - 2 - 1
16	DMU ARRIVES via Up Line under Fiddle Yard control	2 - 2 - 1
17	45208+ BV + 4 min + BV. DEPARTS	4 - 1

Fig. 16

TRAVERSER OPERATOR INSTRUCTIONS

Move No.	Loco + Train formation	Road No.	Bellcode
1	90310 DEPART tender first + BV + 7 min + BV	5	3
2	DMU ARRIVES	2	2 - 2 - 1
3	45208 DEPART chimney first + BV + 4 min + 3 vans + BV	4	1 - 4
4	90310 ARRIVES + 2 BV's	5	1 - 1 - 3
5	82026+ Inspection Saloon Out and back (Under own control)	2	2 - 2 - 1
6	61161 DEPARTS tender first + Empty Coaching Stock (via UP line)	1	2 - 2 - 1
7	45208 ARRIVES + BV + 3 vans + 2 min + BV	4	1 - 4
8	68935 DEPARTS + Bogie Bolster, 3 Grampus, 2 Dogfish, Mermaid + BV	3	3
9	61161 ARRIVES Light engine	1	2 - 3
10	45208 DEPARTS Propels 2 BV's	4	1 - 1 - 3
11	68935 ARRIVES + Bogie Bolster, Mermaid, 2 Dogfish, 3 Grampus + BV	3	3
12	90310 DEPARTS + 2 BV's (Hauled)	5	1 - 1 - 3
13	61161 DEPARTS LE via UP line	1	2 - 3
14	90310 ARRIVES + BV + 5 MIN + BV	5	4 - 1
15	61161 ARRIVES + Empty Coaching Stock	1	2 - 2 - 1
16	DMU DEPARTS (Under own control)	2	2 - 2 - 1
17	45208 ARRIVES + BV + 4 min + BV	4	4 - 1

Standard commonly used bell codes

Train Entering Section	2
Train Out of Section	2 - 1
Restricted Acceptance	3 - 5 - 5
Opening of signal box	5 - 5 - 5
Closing of signalbox	7 - 5 - 5

page 1, a corresponding change must also be made on page 2 (and vice versa).

In addition to the operating sequence, a set of Supplementary Operating Instructions (see *Fig. 17*) and Signalmen's Instructions (see *Fig. 18*) are provided to give guidance to the operators on how the layout is intended to be operated and also give basic instruction on the correct use of bell codes to be sent between the two operators. By following these instructions it is possible to operate the layout without any verbal dialogue between the operators.

Fig. 17

HALIFAX KING CROSS SUPPLEMENTARY OPERATING INSTRUCTIONS

1.   Station operator to control movements off the traverser.
 Traverser operator to control movements onto the traverser.
 (Except in instruction 9)

2.   All point and signal switches to be returned to Normal (UP) position at the end of each movement.

3.   All freight trains to arrive King Cross via DOWN line and MUST pause at STOP board for approx. 10 seconds before proceeding.

4.   All Passenger. Empty Coaching Stock and parcels trains to arrive King Cross via UP line and MUST run into Main platform.

5.   ALL trains to depart via UP line.

6.   Locos are not permitted to run onto the wagon turntable. 'Reach' wagons to be used to position/collect wagons from warehouse siding.

7.   Traverser operator must disengage bolts on traverser immediately after the arrival of every train and before sending 'Train out of Section' bell code.

8.   To avoid excessive handling of Locos, the DOWN line between the traverser and the STOP board may be used for light engine moves to reposition locos on the traverser table. These movements are to be made under the control of the traverser operator. The Shunt Ahead signal (when illuminated) indicates that the Down line is under the control of the traverser operator.

10   All attempts must be made to maintain a continuous flow of movements on the scenic boards at realistic speeds.

     Most importantly - Enjoy yourself - Spread the message that model railways are fun.

Fig. 18

HALIFAX KING CROSS SIGNALMEN'S INSTRUCTIONS

General

Where working signals are provided to control movements these MUST be used.

To Despatch a train

1   Marshall train to correct formation. Ensure all vehicles are coupled.

2   Set all points.

3   Send call attention (1 beat).

4   When call attention is acknowledged, send correct 'Is line clear for...?' bell code.

5   When 'Is line clear?' bell code is acknowledged, clear signals where appropriate and send train entering section (2 beats). The train is now OK to go forward and will be controlled by the receiving operator.

6   When the train reaches its destination, the 'Train out of section' (2 pause 1) will be received and this should be acknowledged by repetition. Signals should be restored to the Stop position. All point and signal switches to be returned to Normal position.

To Receive a train

1   Call attention (1 beat) will be offered by other Operator. This should be acknowledged even if you are not in a position to accept the train.

2   The 'Is line clear for...?' bell code will be offered. If you are not in a position to accept the train this should not be acknowledged. When able to accept the train, acknowledge the bell code by repeating, set up the route and signals (where-appropriate).

3   'Train entering section' (2 beats) will be offered and should be acknowledged.
 The train can now be driven towards you.

4   When arrived complete (i.e. Brake van at rear complete with tail lamp), send 'Train out of section' bell code (2 pause 1), return all signals to danger, set all points and signals to normal position.

Example 2 – Drighlington and Adwalton

'Drighlington and Adwalton' is a circular layout requiring seven operators and is operated as much as possible in accordance with prototype practice. The trackplan is at *Fig. 19*.

To operate the layout requires four signalmen and three drivers, and duties are strictly divided between the two functions just as on the full-size railway. The four signalmen communicate between each other using block instruments, and the drivers are required to drive in accordance with the signals.

'Drighlington and Adwalton' is a scale model of the actual place which was situated on the former Great Northern Railway route between Bradford and Wakefield. The operating sequence is based on the actual working timetables for the period (circa 1962).

The full timetable sequence is nine pages long and just one sample page is reproduced herewith to show how the information is displayed (see *Fig. 20*). All operators are given an identical copy of the sequence sheets, but only certain sections will be relevant for their particular duties.

The first column on the sequence sheets shows the times that the trains were booked to pass Adwalton Junction. Those times which are displayed with a / symbol (e.g. 09/36) denote passing times.

The second column shows the Train Identity description (TID) or headcode as it is more commonly known, and is a useful means of identifying individual trains. This standard four-digit headcode format was introduced by British Railways in the early 1960s and is still in use today. The first digit of the TID denotes the class of train (1 = express passenger, 2 = ordinary passenger, 3 = parcels, etc.), the second digit identifies the destination area of the train and the last two digits are individual train numbers. Details of these codes are contained in the working timetables.

The third column on the sequence sheets shows the start time, the origin and destination of each train.

The fourth column gives the loco identity. The layout is operated by DCC and the individual loco addresses are taken from the last four digits of the loco number.

The fifth column gives the bell code appropriate to each train to assist the signalmen.

The sixth column indicates which road in the storage sidings each train will start from.

The seventh column identifies which direction the train will travel (up or down) and also whether it will travel via the Main or the Branch line.

The eighth column indicates which road in the storage sidings the train will terminate in.

The final column is for any special notes, instructions or information.

In addition to these train movements, there are also separate rows shown as 'Yard Movement'. These rows are for the information of the fiddle yard driver and signalman. The storage yards are arranged in four distinct groups designated as Wakefield Westgate, Batley and Bradford Exchange for the passenger trains and Ardsley for the freight trains. If a train makes a circuit of the layout travelling from Bradford to Wakefield, for example, its next working will be from Wakefield back to Bradford, and an attempt has been made to replicate the workings of the passenger stock (and locos) as near as possible to the prototype. This requires locos to be turned and run round their trains, preferably without handling and a dedicated shunt driver is rostered to perform these duties.

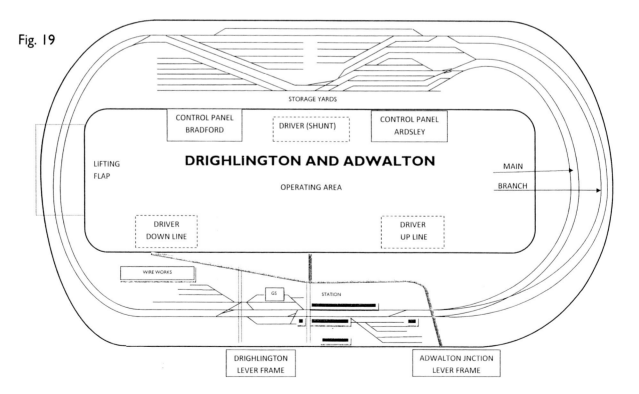

Fig. 19

Drighlington for Adwalton is Steve Hall's latest layout and is seen here under construction. It consists of a continuous circuit, a passing station with goods yard and a double junction. There are also extensive fiddle yards. There are two interlocked mechanical lever frames and communication between operators is by full-size ex-BR block instruments.

STEVE HALL

Drighlington and Adwalton Junction timetable sequence

Fig. 20

TIME	TID	TRAIN	LOCO	BELL CODE	FROM	Adwalton Junction	TO	
09/36	8P60	09:30 Birkenshaw – Dewsbury	68834	3	AR6	UP BRANCH	SLIP	
09/51	1E06	09:03 Halifax - London Kings Cross via Morley	82026	4	BD4	UP MAIN	WD6	SET B
YARD MOVEMENT 82026 turn via cassette, LE to WD4 attach to SET A 68834 from SLIP to WD5. Run round via cassette and attach to Brake van
10/19	3C11	09.45 Wakefield Westgate – Bradford Exchange Parcels Via Batley	42116	1-3-1	BY6	DOWN BRANCH	BD6	(CCT ,CCT, BG,) 42116 Hold at BD6
YARD MOVEMENT 68935 LE 56B to UTL reverse, to A32, reverse, to AR5, attach
10/21	9P17	10:08 Dudley Hill - Ardsley Old Coal Yard (tender first)	64919	4-1	AR3	UP MAIN	AR3	
YARD MOVEMENT 64919 LE via B26 TO WD7 to cassette + hold at 56A
10/31 10/34	2C83	09:55 Wakefield Kirkgate - Bradford Exchange	E50157	3-1	BY3	DOWN BRANCH	BD5	Couple E50157+E51428
10/57	8P24	10.25 Ardsley Spring lane – Bradford Adolphus Street	90310	1-4	AR7	DOWN MAIN	AR7	
YARD MOVEMENT 90310 LE to A35, double reversal to A32 reverse VIA UTL to 56B HOLD
11.14 11.15	2H63	11.00 Bradford Exchange- Hull	E50157 + E51428	3-1	BD5	UP BRANCH	BY3	UNCOUPLE E50157+E51428 DELETE CONSIST
YARD MOVEMENT 64919 LE 56A via A31 + DTL to A35, reverse to AR7. attach
11.20	9P22	09:00 Ardsley Spring lane - Laisterdyke SHUNTS COAL YARD AT DRIGHLINGTON	68935	3	AR5	DOWN MAIN	-	Locked inside for Down Trains to pass.
11/22	1E10	11:05 Bradford Exchange - London Kings X via Batley	61161	4	BD7	UP BRANCH	WD3	SET D
YARD MOVEMENT 61161 Turn Via Cassette LE To WD6, attach
11.29 11.30	2C83	10:55 Wakefield Kirkgate - Bradford Exchange	E51426	3-1	BY2	DOWN BRANCH	BD1	
YARD MOVEMENT 61023 LE 56B via B26, reverse to AR3
11/39	1N03	07:50 London Kings X - Bradford Exchange Via Morley THE WEST RIDING	82026	4	WD4	DOWN MAIN	BD5	SET A
YARD MOVEMENT 82026 Turn on cassette. Hold   68834 Engine + Brake Van WD5 via A31 to SLIP
11/45	0P60	11:30 Dewsbury – Birkenshaw Engine + Brake Van	68834	3	SLIP	DOWN BRANCH	AR6	

Example 3 – Retford

The timetable for Retford is made up from a selection of trains taken from the 1957 summer Working Timetable (WTT). At a major location such as this, it is not possible to run every single train which ran as this would require an enormous fleet of locomotives and rolling stock and impossibly large storage yards. The first step in creating the operating sequence was to create a list of all passenger trains calling at or passing through Retford and put these in time order into an MS Word document. This information was extracted from the Summer 1957 East Coast Main Line Working Timetable which includes details of trains on both the GN and GC routes.

Retford is a very complex layout (see *Fig. 21*) requiring up to eight operators based around the three signal boxes of Retford North, Retford South and Babworth. There are two operators at Retford North who control the points and signals associated with that signal box and also drive trains on the GN circuit, one man driving in the up direction and the other in the down. There are also two operators at Retford South who control the points and signals associated with that box which includes the famous flat crossing where the Great Central line from Manchester to Cleethorpes crosses the East Coast Main Line, just south of Retford station. The Retford South operators also drive trains round the GC

circuit. The Babworth operator is located to the North of Retford station on the GN main line and controls the junction where the lines converge into just two tracks heading north. The Babworth operator also drives some trains between the siding and the extensive fiddle yard. In addition, a shed driver is required for loco movements on/off the loco depot, a yard shunter for shunt moves in the up yard and a 'controller' to co-ordinate all the moves.

Decisions were then made as to which passenger trains would be represented in the sequence, and these trains were then copied and pasted into a new document. Freight trains were then inserted into the gaps between the passenger services to

Retford is Roy Jackson's magnificent project to model this station as it was in the 1960s. Here a northbound passenger train and a southbound freight pass over the famous flat crossing at Retford South signal box.
ANDY YORK / BRITISH RAILWAY MODELLING MAGAZINE

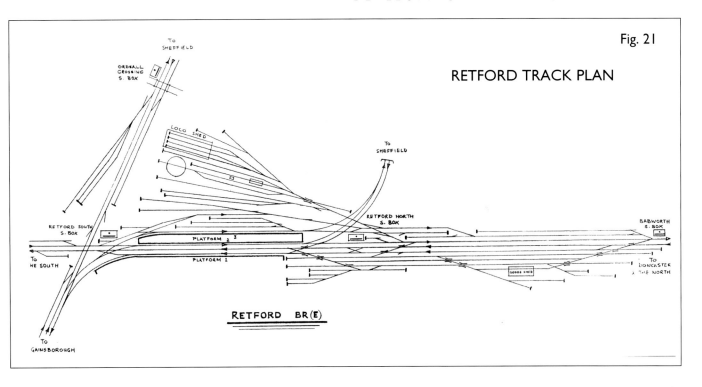

Fig. 21

RETFORD TRACK PLAN

RETFORD BR(E)

create more even flow of movements throughout the day. Some additional movements were also added for light engine movements on and off Retford (GN) shed and also to replicate the constant flow of light engine moves which passed over the flat crossing between Retford GC shed and the yards at Worksop, often two or three locos coupled together.

The first versions of the operating sequence was simply a list of trains to run in time order, but this was found to be inadequate due to the complexity of the layout and it became obvious that more detailed instructions were required to help the operators. The simple list of train movements evolved into the detailed Operating Cards that are in use today and these contain information as to which fiddle yard road the train starts/ends in with the corresponding lever numbers, which controller to use and which point and signal numbers to throw (see *Fig. 22*). The cards are colour coded, with green for Retford North, blue for Retford South, yellow for moves which involve both, and pink for Babworth. Instructions for shunting movements are also included on the cards, giving as much information as possible to assist the operators.

The sequence has evolved and grown over the past ten years to over 100

individual movements. Initially four copies of the operating cards were printed out and inserted into folders for Retford North, Retford South and Babworth operators and also a copy for the controller. This became a mammoth task, however, requiring reams of paper which soon became obsolete when the next updated version of the sequence was

introduced. Computers are now used at each operating position with the latest version of the Operating Cards loaded in from a memory card at the start of each running session. A fourth (slave) screen is also provided on the outside of the layout so that visitors are informed of what trains are operating.

Fig. 22

RETFORD OPERATING CARDS   VERSION 23

MOVE No.	TIME	TRAIN DESCRIPTION
1	03:19 Arrival	01.48 Leeds- Retford Class C Parcels (SK, 3BG, B)

Fiddle yard Road	Levers	CONTROL
GN UP 11	1, 6, 11	GN UP MAIN

POINTS	N34
SIGNALS	
BABWORTH	N5 (Yard Panel)

INSTRUCTIONS
Terminates Platform 1.
RESTORE N34
SWITCH PLATFORM 1 to UP SLOW CONTROLLER
RESTORE FIDDLE YARD 6 & 11
REVERSE N6 & N5 (Yard Panel)
SET BACK TO NO. 1 UP SIDING
ATTACH BS,CL,S,BS (off 20.54 arrival)
RESTORE N6 & N5 (Yard Panel)

TRAIN SIGNALS.

125. For the information of Station-masters, Signalmen, and others, each engine must carry the prescribed Head Lamps or Discs, and Destination Boards where provided.

Distinctive Head Lamps, Discs, and Boards.

126. Every train travelling on the Line must have a Tail Lamp, properly cleaned and trimmed, attached to the last vehicle, by day as well as by night. The Lamp need not be lighted in the daytime, except in foggy weather or during falling snow, or where otherwise provided, but its presence in the rear of each passing train will furnish evidence to the Signalmen that no portion of the train has become detached.

Tail Lamp to indicate last vehicle.

Tail, Side, and Head Lights, after sunset, and in foggy weather or falling snow.

127. (a) After sunset, and in foggy weather or during falling snow, every engine must carry the necessary Head Lights, and, when running alone, a Red Tail Light also; and, except as shown in the following paragraph, or where instructions are issued to the contrary, every train while on any Running Line must carry a Red Tail Light on the last vehicle, and two Red Side Lights.

Head, Side and Tail Lamps on Parallel Lines.

(b) Where trains are run in the same direction on Parallel Lines, special Regulations for Head, Side, and Tail Lamps will be made, when necessary, to meet the circumstances of each case.

Guard to see that Tail and Side Lamps are burning.

(c) The Guard, if there be only one, or the rear Guard, if there be more than one, must see that the Tail and Side Lamps are kept properly burning when necessary.

Engine Tail Lamp.

128. (a) Engines when on any Running Line without a train must carry a Tail Lamp in the rear both by day and by night.

(b) Engines assisting trains in the rear must carry a Tail Lamp.

(c) Engines drawing trains must not carry any Tail Lamp in the rear.

(d) In the case of two or more engines running coupled together without a train, the last engine only must carry a Tail Lamp.

Shunting engines.

129. Shunting engines employed exclusively in Station Yards and Sidings must, after sunset or in foggy weather or during falling snow, carry both Head and Tail Lamps showing a Red Light or such other Light as may be prescribed.

130. (a) An additional Tail Lamp or a Red Board or a Red Flag by day, or an additional Red Tail Light by night, carried on the last vehicle of a train or on an engine, indicates that a Special train is to follow; but the additional Tail Signal need not be carried by preceding trains for Special trains of which previous printed or written notice has been given.

Specials following.

Specials run under notice.

(b) A printed or written notice of Special trains must be given when practicable; but when such trains have to run at short notice, and the issue of a printed or written advice is impossible, the train must be telegraphed from the starting point to the necessary Stations in advance. The staff must at all times be prepared for extra trains.

Specials run without notice.

(c) The Station-master or person in charge at the starting point of a Special Passenger train, of the running of which no previous printed or written notice has been given, must, when practicable, take care that the additional Tail Signal is affixed on the last vehicle of the preceding train, and he must inform the Guard in charge of it of the description and destination of the Special train. The Guard of the train preceding the Special train must inform the person in charge of each Station at which he stops of the description and destination of the train that is following, and take care that the additional Tail Signal is removed from his own train when no longer wanted.

Special Passenger train following.

(d) Relief trains, if run without previous printed or written notice, must be considered and treated as Special trains.

Relief trains.

Slip Carriage Signals.

131. (a) When Slip Carriages are run on a train the indications must be as follow:—

If there be only one Slip portion ... ...

One Red and one White Tail Light, placed side by side on the rear of the Slip portion, thus:—

If there be two separate Slip portions on the same train ...

One Red and one White Tail Light, placed vertically on the rear of the portion first to be Slipped, thus:—

One Red and one White Tail Light, placed side by side on the second or inner Slip portion thus:—

By day the Lamps must be encircled by Discs of the same colour as the Lights shown by night.

(b) The Slip portion, or the first carriage where there is more than one to be slipped at the same Station, must, after dusk and in foggy weather or during falling snow, carry a White Head Light, in order that after the Slip portion has been detached, Signalmen and others may see it approaching.

White Head Light to be carried on Slip portion.

NOTE.—*In addition to the Tail Lamps, as above, each set of "Slips" must carry the usual Side Lamps.*

For Regulations for Working Slip Carriages see Appendix X.

WORKING OF TRAINS.

132. The Engine-driver and Fireman must be with their engine at such time previous to the starting of the train as the Locomotive Superintendent may require, and they must satisfy themselves that their engine is in proper order.

Time of attendance.

Engine to be in proper order.

133. The Engine-driver must have with him on his engine or tender a complete set of Lamps, a box of not less than twelve Detonators, two Red Flags, a Fire-bucket, and such tools as may be ordered by the Locomotive Superintendent.

Articles to be taken.

134. Except where otherwise provided, no engine must be allowed to be in motion on any Running Line unless both the Engine-driver and Fireman are upon it.

Engine not to be in motion on Running line without Driver and Fireman being upon it

135. The Driver and Fireman, when on duty, must not leave their engine unless it is absolutely necessary for them to do so, nor, except as directed in the Rules, without a man being left in charge of it, or the engine is in a Siding and out of gear with the Hand-break hard on.

Driver and Fireman not to leave engine.

CHAPTER FIVE

RULES AND REGULATIONS

What did the real railway do?

Real railways developed detailed books of rules and regulations which company staff (or servants as they were termed) would be obliged to learn. These rules covered all aspects of working the railway from signals to the working of trains and the importance of keeping station clocks to time. They did this for good reason: the real railway works through teamwork and everyone - from drivers to signalmen and from station staff to goods office clerks – had to know what everyone else was doing.

Each Pre-Grouping railway company had its own rule book and these were superseded by ones for the LMS, LNER, GWR and SR and then by the 1950 British Railways edition which was revised in 1962 and 1972.

In addition to the rule books there were a number of other important documents which railway servants had to be familiar with:

- Regional appendix
- Rules for train signalling
- Sectional appendix
- Working timetables
- Carriage working books
- Classification and marshalling of freight trains
- Station instructions

Operating the railway relied on the co-operation and team-working of a great many people. Railways can be dangerous places, for the staff and for the travelling public. Take the simple task of running a train into a terminus, uncoupling, running round, and recoupling. This was an activity that happened many times, but, proportionally, very few railway servants were injured. That was because at each stage, each person knew what the other was doing, and how they would indicate that they had finished their job. So getting between the coaches and engine to uncouple and disconnect the hoses could be life-threatening, yet the driver knew that he was waiting for the hand signal to indicate that the fireman had uncoupled the train before moving forward. Before any movement, the driver would sound his whistle/horn to warn others of his intentions.

One of the most well-known rules from the BR Rule Book was Rule 55, which obliged the fireman of any train brought to a stand at a stop signal for more than two minutes to inform the signalman of its presence, either by walking to the box and speaking to him or, in later days, using a telephone. This important rule was introduced to ensure that a busy signalman could not forget about a train standing in a block section and allow another train into that section.

To give two other examples, Rule 127 says (amongst other things) that a driver 'must regulate the running of his engine to ensure, as far as practicable, punctual working, care being taken to avoid excessive speed'. Another clause says: 'when running through junctions to or from lines diverging from the straight road, (the driver must) regulate the speed to ensure a steady passage for the whole train through the junction points and crossings'.

The key thing is that the real railway expected its servants to be competent at the job they were to do and so they tested their staff on these rules. The staff of the Great Western, for example, ran Mutual Improvement Classes and many companies had a railway institute or similar where training took place.

A good book for everyone to read is L.T.C. Rolt's *Red for Danger*; this sets out how the rule book changed over time as the railway companies learned from experience and accidents.

Rules are set out in the rule book and expanded on in the General Appendix.

This scene at St. Asaph on the Rhyl-Denbigh line in the early 1950s shows three railwaymen following the rule book to get the train away. The fireman of ex-LMS 2-6-2T No. 41232 is seen looking back along the train waiting for the 'Right Away' from the guard, a porter was helping load two bicycles onto the train, while the Station Master was making sure all the doors were properly closed.   MILEPOST 92 ½

This is the book to turn to for the correct way to load wagons, for example. In addition, each section of line was governed by particular regulations set out in the Appendix to the Working Timetables. These covered the location of signal boxes and water troughs, the severity of gradients and the type of signalling systems used on different sections of route. To give an extreme example, the diminutive L&NWR terminus at Holywell Town in North Wales was at the top of a 1 in 27 gradient. The Appendix to the Working Timetable specified that passenger trains, which were push-pull operated, should always have the locomotive at the rear of the train when heading up the gradient and at the head of the train when descending, to ensure that maximum braking power was available. Goods trains were treated similarly and had to be propelled up the incline, with a brake van at either end, and were limited to three loaded goods or mineral wagons or five empty ones in either direction.

How can we replicate this in model form?
In the preface I said this would not be a book of 'thou shalt not', but having some rules and regulations on model railway can add to the enjoyment of operation, For example, you could specify that there is a limit to the number of wagons that can be conveyed by your goods trains due to some imaginary gradient off scene. If there are more wagons to be moved than

the limit allows, you will have to run an additional goods train to clear the traffic. This is exactly what happened in real life. Another limiting factor could be a bridge with a weight restriction which would mean only locomotives with a light axle loading could be used on the line.

Having an agreed set of rules about the way a layout should be operated also helps a team to present a layout at an exhibition. See Steve Hall's Halifax King Cross Supplementary Operating Instructions' in the chapter on timetables.

I recommend getting hold of the Rule Book for your favoured railway company at your chosen period; it will give you many insights into how the real railway worked and how you should run the trains on your layout.

A good example of using the rule book is on Tim Venton's 'Clutton' layout. This uses the correct bell codes to offer and describe trains which run under

the control of fixed signals. These signals are only released by the route being correctly set. Signals are used exclusively to control the trains and the roles of driver and signalman are quite distinct. The person who sets the route does not drive. This helps ensure that mistakes are minimised. Where movements take place other than under fixed signals, gestures are made to indicate readiness of moves.

For Tim it is important that the rule book is followed, as this ensures that trains run correctly. On his layout, trains carry head codes and tail lamps and a sequence timetable is used. Observation of the real trains at Clutton means the trains are accurate representations of the real ones. Unfortunately, this does lead to a layout that polarises opinion; some find it 'boring', while others find it very interesting. For Tim, the fact that so many professional railway people can be entertained is just reward.

Eccleston Gas Works operating rules

The Eccleston Gas Works locomotive may propel no more than three wagons along the Down Line from the Gas Works Siding to Eccleston Station. The same locomotive may haul no more than three wagons in the wrong direction along the Down Line from Eccleston Station to the Gas Works Siding. These workings do not require a brake van.

These moves will be made under the control of Eccleston Station Signal Box. The signalman on duty must obtain permission from Croston Sidings Signal Box by using the 'Blocking Back Inside Home Signal' bell code (2-4) and, when the train is safely in the sidings at Eccleston or the Gas Works, sending the 'Obstruction Removed' bell code (2-1).

I have imagined that there is a small gas works with its own siding just 'off scene' on my layout and drawn up these rules for how it should be worked.

84

ENGINE HEAD LAMPS.

The following uniform system of Head Lamps is adopted by all Railway Companies running over the Lancashire and Yorkshire Railway, and on those Lines over which the Lancashire and Yorkshire Company's engines run. The Lamps must be carried both by day and night in the positions indicated, and at night or in foggy weather show White Lights only.

1. Express Passenger Train, Break-Down Van Train going to clear the line, or Light Engine going to assist disabled Train.

(Bell Signal, 4 beats consecutively.)

2. Ordinary Passenger Train, or Break-Down Van Train not going to clear the line.

(Bell Signal, 3—1.)

3. Fish, Meat, Fruit, Horse, Cattle, or Perishable Train composed of Coaching Stock.

(Bell Signal, 5 beats consecutively.)

4. Empty Coaching Stock Train.

(Bell Signal, 2—2—1.)

5. Fish, Meat, or Fruit Train composed of Goods Stock, Express Cattle, or Express Goods Train, Class "A."

(Bell Signal, 3—2.)

6. Express Cattle, or Express Goods Train, Class "B."

(Bell Signal, 1—4.)

85

ENGINE HEAD LAMPS—continued.

7. Light Engine or Light Engines coupled together, or Engine and Break.

(Bell Signals, 2—3 and 1—3—1.)

8. Through Goods, Mineral, or Ballast Train.

Bell Signal, 4—1.)

9. Ordinary Goods or Mineral Train stopping at intermediate Stations.

(Bell Signal, 3 beats consecutively.)

Distinctive Head Lamps for Electric Trains.

During the daytime, Electric Trains will carry white discs instead of head and tail lamps. When dark, lamps will be carried as usual.

Distinctive Head Lamps for Pilot Engines running between Aintree Sorting Sidings and Liverpool Stations.

The Liverpool Pilot Engines will be distinguished by Head Lamps as under—the lamps will be carried both by day and night in the positions indicated, and at night, or in foggy weather, will show White Lights only:—

GREAT HOWARD STREET.   NORTH DOCKS.   NORTH MERSEY.   BANKFIELD.

44

ENGINE HEAD LAMPS.

All L.M.S. engines, whether working over the L.M.S. or other Companies' lines, and the engines of other Companies working over the L.M.S. lines, must, unless instructions are issued to the contrary, carry white head lights arranged as under, and trains must be signalled by the bell signals shown:—

Description of train.	Bell Signal.	Head Light.
1.—Express passenger train, or break-down van train going to clear the line, or light engine going to assist disabled train, or fire brigade train...	4	
2.—Ordinary passenger train, or break-down van train not going to clear the line...	3—1	
Branch passenger train (where authorised)	1—3	
Rail motor or motor train with engine leading	3—1—2	
(When running with driving compartment leading rail motors or motor trains will carry the headlamp on the same bracket as used for the tail lamp.)		
NOTE.—For arrangements in regard to electric trains see the various electric line instruction books.		
3.—Parcels, newspaper, fish, meat, fruit, milk, horse, or perishable train, composed of coaching stock	1—1—3	
4.—Empty coaching stock train	2—2—1	
Fitted freight, fish or cattle train with the continuous brake in use on NOT LESS than one-third the vehicles ...	5	
5.—Express freight or cattle train with the continuous brake on less than one-third the vehicles, but in use on four vehicles connected to the engine indicated by ✠ in the Working Time Tables	2—2—3	
Express freight or cattle train not fitted with the continuous brake, or with the continuous brake in use on LESS than four vehicles	3—2	
6.—Through freight train, or ballast train conveying workmen and running not less than 15 miles without stopping	1—4	
7.—Light engine, or light engines coupled together	2—3	
Engine with one or two brakes	1—3—1	
8.—Through mineral or empty wagon train	4—1	
9.—Freight train stopping at intermediate stations, or ballast train running short distance	3	
Branch freight train (where authorised)	1—2	
Ballast train, freight train, or officers' special requiring to stop in section or at intermediate siding in section	1—2—2	
10.—Shunting engines working exclusively in station yards and sidings.		Must, whilst in those sidings, carry one red head light and one red tail light.

The lamps must be carried in position day and night.

NOTE.—Local exceptional arrangements are shown in the respective Sectional Appendices. When a train running on the L.M.S. Railway is worked by two engines attached in front of the train, the second engine must not carry head lamps.

Head lamp codes used by the LMS taken from the LMS General Appendix to the Working Time Tables 1937.
MIKE FITTON COLLECTION

Left: *L&YR rules relating to head and tail lamps.*
L&YR Rules and Regulations 1908,
LYRS COLLECTION

DOWN TRAINS—Week Days.

Fig. 23

3.0 a.m. from Euston.

(Newspaper Train.)

	Balanced at
Break Van (45 ft.) ⎫	
Sorting Van (X) ⎪	
Two Newspaper Vans (X) ⎬ Birmingham	A
Break Van (X) ⎪	
Parcel Sorting Van (X)—Coventry	A
Break Van (X)—Liverpool	7 15 a.m.
Break Van (X)—Carlisle	—

Rugby to attach in front Third Class and Composite and despatch for Birmingham at 4.34 a.m.

The Carlisle van to be detached at Acton Bridge and attached to the 5.50 a.m. from Crewe for Preston, to go forward thence by 9.2 a.m. train to Carlisle.

A Locally to Rugby and 7.20 p.m. thence to Euston.

9.2 a.m. from Preston.

(8.5 a.m. from Liverpool, L. & Y.)

(7.55 a.m. from Manchester, L. & Y.)

(7.45 a.m. from Liverpool (Lime Street), Mondays only.)

(8.0 a.m. from Manchester (Exchange), Mondays only.)

	Balanced at
Break Van ⎫	
Third Class (X) ⎪ Liverpool (L.&Y.)	1D40 p.m.
Tri Composite (42 ft.) ⎬ to Carlisle	
Tri Composite (42 ft.) ⎭	
A Break Van (X) {London to Carlisle	—
Tri Composite ⎱ Liverpool (L.&Y.)	8B30 a.m.
Break Carriage (42 ft.) ⎰ to Windermere	
M Third Class ⎱ Liverpool (L. St.)	—
M Tri Composite ⎰ to Windermere	
M Break Van ⎱	
M Third Class ⎱ Manchester (Ex.)	8S20 a.m.
M Tri Composite ⎰ to Windermere	
M Break Van ⎰	
C Break Composite ⎱ Manchester (L&Y)	2 20 p.m.
(L. & Y.) (1 & 3) ⎰ to Whitehaven	

Preston to attach two Thirds for Windermere (Mondays and Saturdays excepted). | 4 15 ,,

On Mondays and Saturdays the 7.55 a.m. from Manchester (L. & Y.) will convey the following through Vehicles for Windermere to be run through independently of the 9.2 a.m. from Preston, being made up as follows :—

†Break Third (L. & Y.) ⎫	
Third Class (L. & Y.) ⎬ Manchester (L.&Y.)	6 35 p.m.
Composite (L. & Y.) ⎪ to Windermere	
Break Third (L. & Y.) ⎭	
Break Composite (L. & Y.) ⎱ Manchester (L.&Y.)	2 20 ,,
(L. & Y.) ⎰ to Whitehaven	

A Leaves London 3.0 a.m., and is attached at Acton Bridge to the 5.50 a.m. from Crewe for Preston.

B 8.20 a.m. Saturdays.

C Except Mondays and Saturdays.

D To Lime Street. Works 2.35 a.m., Lime Street to Crewe, and 11.6 a.m. thence to Carlisle.

M Mondays only.

S Saturdays only.

5.0 a.m. from Euston.

	Balanced at
Parcel Van ⎫	8A30 a.m.
‡Brk Tri Compo.(57 ft.) (X) ⎬ Manchester	11B20 ,,
‡Brk. Tri Compo.(57 ft.) (X) ⎫ Liverpool	2 0 p.m.
Tri Composite (57 ft.) (X) ⎭	
M Third Class ⎱ Crewe	—
Post Office (50 ft.) ⎰	3 2 p.m.
Break Van (50 ft.) (X)—Glasgow	5 55 ,,
Break Van (45 ft.)—Crewe (C)	—
Break Van (45 ft.)—Birmingham	11D20 a.m.

Rugby to detach the Birmingham Van, and attach a Birmingham District Twin of 4 equal to 6.

Rugeley to detach the Shrewsbury Van, and send forward at 8.20 a.m.

Stafford to attach through vehicles for Manchester and for Liverpool (Mondays and Saturdays excepted from July 16th to September 12th) off 7.20 a.m. from Birmingham, and despatch at 8.27 a.m.

Crewe to attach a Tri Composite for Manchester daily. | 11 20 a.m.

A To Stoke, and forward locally.

B From Bolton.

D From Walsall.

C Via Shrewsbury. To be labelled Shrewsbury.

M Mondays only.

7.20 a.m. from Birmingham.

	Balanced at
Break Third (57 ft.) (X) ⎱ Manchester	12B10 a.m.
Tri Composite (57 ft.) (X) ⎰	
Composite (W. C. J. S.) ⎫	9E5 p.m
Tri Composite (57 ft.) (X) ⎬ Liverpool (A)	9D0 ,,
Break Third (57 ft.) (X) ⎭	9D0 ,,
C Composite ⎫	
C Third Class ⎬ Blackpool	6 38 ,,
C Break Van ⎭	
H Third Class ⎱ Stafford	11 45 a.m.
Break Van ⎰	—

An extra Third Class to be run for Manchester and Liverpool on Mondays and Saturdays.

A On Saturdays and Mondays from July 16th to September 12th, inclusive, the Liverpool portion will be marshalled in front and extended from Stafford to Liverpool independently, leaving Stafford at 8.22 a.m.

B From London.

C Saturdays and Mondays only until September 12th. Leaves Crewe at 9.38 a.m.

D From London. Works 12.0 noon, Liverpool to London.

E From Glasgow. Works 9.50 a.m., Liverpool to Glasgow, and thence to Birmingham as shown.

H Except Saturdays and Mondays until September 12th, then daily.

Passenger trains were not a random collection of vehicles but carefully planned as shown in this extract from the L&NWR Marshalling Circular for July, August and September 1910.

LNWR SOCIETY

CHAPTER SIX
TRAIN FORMATIONS AND OPERATIONAL INTEREST

What did the real railway do?

Most real trains were not a random collection of vehicles; they were carefully thought out and arranged for passengers and the practical requirements of the railway operating staff. Real trains were identified by headlamps arranged in different patterns according to the type of train involved. Each company had its own set of headlamp codes until they were standardised by the Railway Clearing House and later by BR. Each train also carried a red tail lamp to indicate to signalmen and other staff that it was complete and had not divided between stations or yards.

Passenger trains were made up of vehicles designed to carry different classes of passengers (first, second or third) in proportion to the number of people likely to be travelling in these designations. Restaurant cars were usually placed in the middle of a train to provide access for passengers from all part of the train. Every passenger train, even if it consisted of one coach, had to have a brake compartment for the guard.

Passenger train marshalling books were produced by all the railway companies and *Fig. 23* shows an extract from the L&NWR carriage working book as an example. If you look at the 9.2 a.m. from Preston, you can see that it was made up of carriages which arrived there on four separate trains (two L&NWR and two L&YR) and they were marshalled in the order shown. In addition two Third Class carriages were attached destined for Windermere. As the train made its way north to Carlisle, the carriages for Windermere would be detached (presumably at Oxenholme) and those for Workington would presumably have been detached at Penrith.

There were several different classes of goods trains depending upon the importance and urgency of the traffic. For example, from 1915 the L&YR had four categories: 'Right Away Goods' which were express freights and took precedence even over stopping passenger trains; 'Special Express Merchandise' which

Aspinall 4-4-2 No. 1397 heading an express passenger train over Walkden troughs on the L&YR's main line from Manchester to Liverpool.

Aspinall 2-4-2T No. 643 heading an ordinary passenger train through Mills Hill near Middleton, Manchester.

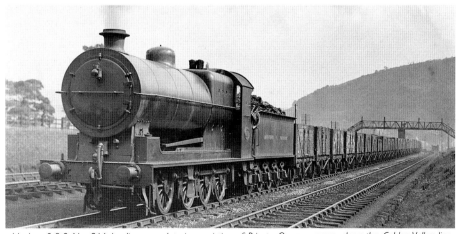

Hughes 0-8-0 No. 216 hauling a coal train consisting of Private Owner wagons along the Calder Valley line through Mytholmroyd. ALL LYRS COLLECTION

An LYR Hoy (rebuilt by Hughes) 0-8-0 No. 408 heading a very short 'Right Away' Goods at Horbury near Wakefield.
LYRS COLLECTION

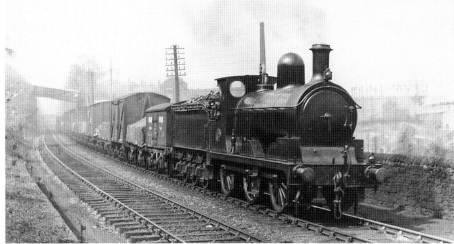

An unidentified LYR Aspinall 0-6-0 heading a 'Special Express Merchandise' train near Halifax.   LYRS COLLECTION

A small-boilered LYR Aspinall 0-8-0 with an 'Express Merchandise' train at Middleton near Manchester.

LYRS COLLECTION

conveyed perishable traffic such as fish, meat and fruit; 'Express Merchandise' which conveyed other urgent traffic; and 'Merchandise' which conveyed everything else. In addition, there were mineral trains for conveying coal, etc. Each category of train was identified by the headlamp code displayed on the locomotive.

In later years goods trains were classified according to how many vacuum-braked wagons were in the train and, for example, the LMS 1937 train classification is shown on page 41. Again each category had its own headlamp code.

Most goods trains were assembled in the same sequence as the goods yards they would visit on their journey to make shunting easier at each location. *Fig. 24* is an extract from *British Railways Classification of Freight Trains, London Midland Region (North Western Lines)* dated 9th September 1963. If you look at the first example, train 7L20 the 1.10 a.m. Mondays Excepted Lostock Hall to Accrington, it would leave Lostock Hall sidings marshalled in the order shown: wagons for Blackburn, wagons for Accrington (which might be moving on to other destinations) and wagons for Accrington itself ('Proper') plus fish vans from Wyre Dock at Fleetwood. The train would stop at Bamber Bridge to attach wagons from there, then when it got to Blackburn it would detach the wagons for that town before moving on to Accrington Exchange Sidings where it would detach wagons destined for other destinations, and finally to Accrington South where it would position the remainder of its train in the goods yard as required. You can follow other examples if you wish.

The main exceptions to this were some branch line goods trains or transfer workings between yards in urban areas which often would be a random collection of wagons working from one goods yard to another.

How can we replicate this in model form?
There is no substitute here for the careful study of photographs of real trains in or around your chosen location and at the appropriate period. Luckily we are blessed with an active railway publishing industry which keeps on churning out tempting new volumes on just about every part of

In LMS days an ex-LYR Aspinall 0-6-0ST works a 'Merchandise' train near Luddendenfoot in the Calder Valley.
LYRS COLLECTION

Fig. 24

- 29 -

7L20 1.10am MX Lostock Hall to Accrington.
1. Blackburn
2. Accrington
3. Accrington Proper & Fish Vans from Wyre Dock.
At Bamber Bridge: Attach
At Blackburn: Detach (1) and attach.
At Accrington Ex. Sdgs: Detach (2)
At Accrington South: Position (3) in Goods Yard, as required.

7J82 1.20am MO Lostock Hall to Royton Jn.
1. Farington Jn.
2. Bolton
3. Bury
4. Broadfield
5. Castleton
6. Rochdale
7. New Hey Proper
8. Royton Jn.
At (1) (2) (3) (5) & (6): detach and attach
At (4)(7) and (8): detach

7L11 9.30am Dly Lostock Hall to Heysham Moss Sdgs.
1. Lancaster B.R.O.
2. Heysham Moss Sdgs. & Middleton Rd. traffic only.
At Preston (Ribble Sdgs): Attach
At Lancaster: Detach (1)
Not to convey from Preston more than 35 wagons and two brakes for Heysham Moss Sdgs.

7L13 10/27pm SX Lostock Hall to Carnforth.
1. Furness
2. Stations to Windermere and Morecambe.
3. Carnforth Proper
At Ribble Sdgs: Attach.

6M12 8/55pm SX Low Moor to Aintree
Arrives on N.W. Lines Marshalled
1. Wigan N.W.
2. Rose Grove (inc. P.& W. Line and Carnforth).
3. Aintree
At Rose Grove: Detach (2) and attach.
At Blackburn T. St: Detach (1) and attach. District Controls concerned to advise forward number of Aintree wagons on train and Preston District Control to advise S.M. Blackburn.

7H14 11.22am Dly Macclesfield to Heaton Mersey.
1. Bollington (SO)
2. Portwood
3. George's Road
4. Heaton Mersey Exch.
At Bollington (SO): Detach (1) and attach.
At Portwood: Detach (2) and attach.
At George's Rd: Detach (3)

7H75 3/ 5pm SO Macclesfield to Newcastle Jn.
1. Longport
2. Etruria
3. Cliff Vale
4. Stoke Yard
At Congleton: Detach and attach.
At Longport: Detach (1) and attach.
At Etruria: Detach (2) and attach
Limited to 20 vehicles between Macclesfield and Congleton.

9H91 6/25pm SX Macclesfield to Stoke.
1. Willesden
2. Stoke South
3. Stoke North
At Congleton: Attach
At Longport: Attach
Limited to 20 vehicles between Macclesfield and Congleton.

4V76 6/25pm SO Manchester London Rd. to Banbury.
1. Banbury Exchange. (incl. Paddington,Pk. Royal, Acton, Greenford, South Lambeth).
2. Oxford
3. Basingstoke
4. Moreton Cutting
5. Crewe Gresty Green Exchange (incl. Birmingham W.R. Worcester, Leamington).
At Crewe G.G: Detach (5)

4A00 8/13pm SX Manchester London Road to Camden.
Camden and Exchange (incl. important goods for Willesden Goods).

4007 8/45pm SX Manchester London Rd. to Basingstoke.
1. Paddington
2. Basingstoke Exch.
3. Moreton Cutting Ex.
4. Crewe G.G. Exch. (incl. Birmingham W.R. Worcester, Leamington, Banbury Exchange (incl. Swindon, Old Oak Common, Park Royal).
At Crewe G.G. Detach (4) and attach.

5B75 9/13pm SX Manchester London Rd. to Nuneaton.
1. Coventry fitted
2. Burton fitted
3. Nottingham (Carrington St).
4. Shed fitted.

5. Willesden fitted
6. Willesden non-fitted
7. Nuneaton Ex. (incl. Tamworth).
8. Rugby Exch.
At Stockport: Attach Nottingham and Northampton traffic at * and also attach other traffic in marshalled order.
At Tutbury: Detach (2) and (3) and attach.
Note: May be made up with not more than 10 Willesden Exch. i. required.
Limited to 50 wagons from Tutbury.

Having run round its train, Aspinall 2-4-2T No. 724 waits to depart with an ordinary passenger train for Preston.   SIMON EDMUNDS

Aspinall 2-4-2T No. 724 has arrived with a passenger train from Preston, run-round and is about to detach a horsebox from the rear of the train.   SIMON EDMUNDS

Britain's fascinating railway network and looking through them is no chore!

For example, when deciding on the formation of the passenger train for Eccleston, I looked at dozens of photographs of L&YR branch passenger trains from my chosen period (c.1910). I concluded that the most likely formation was an Aspinall 2-4-2T hauling a train of five Attock six-wheeled coaches. Luckily, kits for my chosen loco and stock were readily available.

Similarly for goods trains, a study of photographs revealed the typical sort of wagons to be found on a branch line like mine: mostly L&YR open merchandise wagons with some vans and a smattering of similar vehicles from other railway companies which served the North of England, like the L&NWR and the Midland. Similar research would reveal the formation of passenger and goods trains in the Grouping and BR periods.

Such research should ideally be carried out when you are planning your layout as you can then acquire the appropriate kits and build yourself appropriate trains without wasting time and money on locos and stock which would be out of place on your line.

You will need to consider what sort of trains would have served your area and here a study of working timetables is the best source of information. As explained in Chapter 2, these can be obtained from line societies and organisations such as the Public Record Office at Kew or the National Railway Museum at York. To work out the sort of trains which would have served Eccleston, I looked at a number of L&YR branch line WTTs published in branch line booklets published by the L&YR Society. These revealed a straightforward pattern of ordinary passenger trains flowing backwards and forwards along the branch each day; excursion or special trains were not listed as they would have been covered by special traffic notices. Goods services were more complex with two or three locomotives often visiting the line at different times and light engine (or light engine and brake van) movements quite common. I have tried to replicate this in the pattern of services I have developed for Eccleston.

Branch passenger trains often conveyed non-passenger coaching stock, such as

LBSCR E1 0-6-0T No. 135 (ex-Foligno) shunts a four-wheeled brake van into the bay platform at Plumpton Green before working a horsebox special. Plumpton is, of course, well-known for its racecourse.   BARRY LUCK

In this busy scene on John Thompson's layout Lowbum Park, an NER Class P 0-6-0 waits at the signal with an empty mineral train, a train of wagons stands in one of the goods loops, and in the background an NER Class 290 0-6-0T arrives with a transfer working from the riverside branch.   STEVE FLINT, CTY. RAILWAY MODELLER

Calder Bridge Gas Works loco No. 3 Topsy leaves Calder Bridge with a loaded mineral train.   BARRY NORMAN

horseboxes, covered carriage trucks or fish vans. These add variety to operation and interest to shunting.

Larger layouts could feature other types of passenger train, such as semi-fast or express services. Operational interest can be added to these by strengthening them with additional vehicles or splitting them into separate portions at junction stations. This was common practice in steam days and even now continues at some locations using diesel or electric multiple units.

Goods train operation offers a much greater variety of types of train and shunting. Indeed the shunting of goods wagons creates almost infinite variety and can occupy many happy hours! However, it is difficult in model form to accurately re-create shunting of goods wagons on the prototype which mostly consisted of 'loose' shunting where a wagon or group of wagons was given a push by the shunting engine and allowed to run freely into the appropriate siding. We have to push our wagons in as well as pull them out, which is one of the compromises with reality that we have to make.

Other types of train which can be used to create operational variety and interest are parcels trains, engineering trains, breakdown trains and inspection or Directors' saloons. Parcels workings often attracted an interesting mixture of vans, former passenger coaches, brake vans, etc, although they were more common on main lines between major centres than on country branch lines. Engineering wagons carrying rail and ballast were often positioned in sidings where they were needed during the week in readiness for weekend possessions. Breakdown trains could obviously be seen anywhere from time to time and detailed models of breakdown cranes are very attractive. Inspection or Directors' saloons could also pop up unexpectedly anywhere on the network as required and they would often stop in a section to allow for a close look at the track or a bridge and this would delay other traffic. They were usually

An ex-LMS 'Jinty' 0-6-0T hauling a brake van through a rural scene. Engine and brake van moves were very common.
AUTHOR'S COLLECTION

Ex-L&NWR 5ft 6in 2-4-2T taking water at Bangor locomotive shed in June 1947. This typical scene was repeated hundreds of times a day in steam days. Our model steam locos should also 'take water' from time to time.
R. S. CARPENTER COLLECTION

propelled which makes an interesting and unusual move.

And finally, don't forget light engines; these were much more common on real railways than you might think. Locos released from trains arriving at terminal stations or goods yards had to run light to the nearest locomotive depot for turning and servicing, with balancing movements in return. Locos also ran light to main locomotive works for major overhauls or to collect stock from carriage sidings, for example. Wherever possible, two or more light engines would run coupled together and this also makes an interesting move.

Engine and brake van movements were common too; a goods train would arrive at its destination and the wagons

Engine sheds and turntables can add operational interest to a layout. Here L&YR Aspinall 0-6-0ST No. 753 and an NER 0-6-0 share the coal stage outside the engine shed at Calder Bridge.
BARRY NORMAN

L&YR Barton Wright 0-6-0 No. 952 on the turntable at Calder Bridge.   BARRY NORMAN

A BR WD 2-8-0 clanks slowly into Halifax King Cross towing a brake van, no doubt ready to pick up some empty minerals wagons.

TONY WRIGHT

would be shunted into the appropriate sidings. Sometimes a loco would pick up another train and depart hauling that, but if no other train was ready, it would often couple to the brake van and run to another location where it was needed next.

Another source of operational interest is private sidings and the exchange of traffic between them and mainline services. Private sidings can range in size from extensive systems serving a colliery or steelworks to a simple siding serving a factory or loading bank. Again a study of railway books about your chosen area will give you some idea of the sort of industries to be found there.

Most major stations had a station pilot or two to shunt carriages, parcels vans, horseboxes, etc, perhaps to another platform or to sidings to await their next move. Most finescale layouts are not big enough to warrant such a luxury, but if your system includes a large station, it certainly would be worth including. Carriage sidings are also rarely modelled, but they were common in most urban areas. The only layout I have seen them on is 'The Gresley Beat', Cliff Parsons' wonderful evocation of the approaches to King's Cross. If you have space for them they can also add operational interest.

Headlamps

Having the correct head and tail lamps on models enhances their authenticity but changing some lamps in 4mm scale or smaller is a real challenge. It is easier in 7mm scale or larger where the model lamps are easier to handle. On my layout my locos carry lamps which are suitable for their most typical duties, e.g. my 0-6-0ST carries lamps indicating that it is working a Pilot Goods. This is fine when it is hauling such a train or shunting, but when it is running Light Engine (or Light Engine and brake van) it really should carry different lamps. I am afraid that I just turn a blind eye to this anomaly.

This photo was taken at Manchester Exchange, the L&NWR station which was next to the L&YR's Victoria station. It shows L&YR Barton Wright 0-6-2T No. 273, acting as Victoria station pilot, shunting a 12-wheeled Caledonian Railway carriage which was presumably a through carriage from Scotland to somewhere in the North of England. In the background is what looks like an L&NWR tender loco and a carriage truck. This is the sort of interchange between three different companies which makes the Pre-Grouping railway scene so fascinating.
LYRS COLLECTION

An Aspinall 0-6-0 heading a Through Goods or Mineral train at Poulton with the loco displaying three lamps as shown in the list of 1908 headlamps codes shown on page 41.   LYRS COLLECTION

My own model of an Aspinall 0-6-0 displaying the same lamps.   AUTHOR

RUNNING ROUND SEQUENCE

This sequence of four photos shows the process of running round a passenger train. They were taken at Oxenhope, the terminus of the Keighley and Worth Valley Railway in Yorkshire and show the preserved L&YR Barton Wright 0-6-0 No. 957 arriving at the station, running round and coupled to the other end of the train. AUTHOR

A close-up look at the couplings and brake pipes connecting an ex-LNER 'Quint Art' set of stock and the loco at Bethnal Green in May 1956. H. F. WHEELLER COLLECTION

Right: The fireman has gone between the loco and carriage to uncouple and disconnect the vacuum brake hose. The guard has left his lamp on the platform ready to put on the rear of the train. AUTHOR

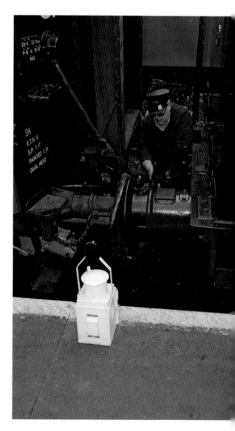

CHAPTER SEVEN
REALISTIC MOVEMENT

What did the real railway do?

Real trains moved purposefully in stations, goods yard and loco depots – the sort of locations most often featured on model railways. They started slowly as the loco took up the weight of the train and, in most cases, accelerated gradually to the speed limit for the section of line they were on. I remember watching express passenger trains setting off from Preston, often in the rain, their wheels slipping as the loco struggled to get going on wet rails, or goods trains pulling out of the yards at Lostock Hall and weaving their way slowly across the points and crossings to get onto the main line; only when the bulk of the train was across the points did the driver open the regulator and attempt to build up speed.

Trains approaching a station, junction or terminus would need to slow down to the appropriate line speed and this could take some time if, for example, the train was a heavy unfitted goods train. Shunting and light engine movements in goods yards, engine sheds and around stations took place purposefully but at relatively slow speeds to ensure the safety of railway staff who might be working there.

Everything took longer than you might think: for example, a simple movement like the arrival and departure of a passenger train at a branch terminus was not a quick affair. The train would arrive at the platform and there would be a pause while the passengers got out of the carriages. The loco crew might have a chat with the station staff while this was going on. Then the fireman would climb down between the loco and the carriages to uncouple the brake pipes, possibly steam heating pipes as well and, finally, the coupling itself. Once the driver was satisfied that the fireman was safely out of the way, he would draw forward slowly beyond the loco release crossover. Then the points would be changed, either by the signalman in the signal box or by the fireman working a ground frame released by the box. If the latter was the case, the loco might pause after it had cleared the

Aspinall 2-4-2T No. 724 leaves Eccleston with an ordinary passenger train to Preston.   SIMON EDMUNDS

points to allow the fireman to restore the points and clamber back on board. Then the loco would run round its train, passing the carriages, until it was clear of the points at the other end of the loop. Finally, it would run forward and buffer up to the coaches, after which the fireman would once again climb down between the loco and the carriages to couple up. The guard might then perform a brake test to ensure the brakes were working correctly throughout the train and were being controlled from the engine in its new position, although the full brake test was probably only carried out when the coaches were first brought into use at the beginning of their use. In addition to all this, the loco might well take water at some point, depending upon the location of the water column. Then, with a new set of passengers on board, the train was ready for departure.

Thankfully, this simple process, which is so often seen on model layouts, can still be observed on preserved steam railways up and down the country. Next time you visit one of these splendid locations, take the time to watch and maybe time the running-round manoeuvre and note just how long it takes. If you cannot get to a

preserved steam railway, observe the way steam trains move on DVDs or on YouTube.

Of course, express trains picked up speed when out of station limits and ran pretty fast – around 60 mph typically in the steam era. Ordinary passenger trains would run at about 30-40 mph, whilst goods trains were usually much slower. The fastest fully-fitted freights of the Grouping or BR periods would also have travelled at up to 60 mph, with some fish trains attaining 75 mph, but most ordinary goods trains rarely reached 30 mph. Heavy mineral trains or trains of empty mineral wagons plodded along at around 25 mph with only the engine brake and the Guard's brake van to stop them.

How can we replicate this in model form?

My main recommendation for the purposeful operation of model railways is to slow everything down. Far too often model trains are operated at ridiculous speeds, and movements, such as running-round, and coupling and uncoupling, are performed far too quickly. Nothing destroys the illusion of reality as much as trains dashing about and performing movements such as coupling-up to stock

My friend and fellow L&YRS Trustee Noel Coates couples some wagons in the goods yard at Eccleston. I prefer to use three-link and screw couplings rather than automatic ones. Some modellers do not like the 'hand from the sky' which this involves, but I prefer that to automatic couplings which spoil the look of locos and stock and are not always reliable.
AUTHOR

far too quickly. I know there were exceptions to this where, for example, shunting was performed at fast speeds because the crew were anxious to finish their shift and go home, but even then it took longer than you might think and doesn't look right on a model.

Of course, we cannot recreate every aspect of real railway operation in model form, but we can at least indicate that it is happening by introducing pauses between movements. For example, to use the branch terminus example again, bring the train into the station and *pause*, while the passengers get off and the fireman uncouples the loco from the train. Run the loco forward and *pause* while the points are changed. Run the loco over the crossover and *pause* while the points are changed. Buffer up to the coaches and *pause* while the loco is coupled up.

Another thing which destroys the illusion of reality is propelling vehicles not coupled to a locomotive. I have often seen at exhibitions a locomotive run up to a set of coaches and push them along a platform or siding. In reality, the coaches would have their vacuum or air brakes on while they were standing and would need to be coupled up to a locomotive – and the vacuum or air pressure restored – before they could be moved. This also applies to non-passenger coaching stock which was also fitted with continuous brakes.

One of the problems which leads to such unrealistic movement on model railways is the use of automatic couplings. I know this is a controversial area, but to my mind there is no substitute for using three-link or screw couplings. Firstly, it is what the real railway did, and, secondly, it forces you to pause between movements while you couple and uncouple the stock. Such couplings also have the great advantage that you can couple and uncouple anywhere on the layout, not just where the magnets or ramps are placed. I appreciate that in the smaller scales, three-link or screw couplings can be difficult to manipulate, particularly for those whose eyesight is not what it was. But if you use automatic couplings, please remember to include the pauses in your movements.

The purposeful movement of trains can also be enhanced by the use of wagon (or rolling stock) movement systems. The Americans have got this down to a fine art with their system of wagon cards and waybills, but very few British outline layouts seem to use such systems. The simplest system that I am aware of was used by Peter Denny on his 'Buckingham' layout. He put a spot of coloured paint on the solebar of each wagon and produced a chart to show how the wagon movements should take place. For example, when a goods train arrived at his terminus, it brought in all the red wagons and collected all the green ones. This system would work well on most layouts which only feature one station or location.

For more complex systems more sophisticated methods can be used with a roll of dice or computer programs used to generate random wagon movement instructions which then have to be carried out by the operator. For each wagon a card can be created which describes the wagon in a way that would help the operator recognise it (e.g. L&NWR van, grey livery, No. 12345) and a space left where a waybill, describing the destination for the wagon, can be attached with a clip. When a goods train is assembled at a station or in a fiddle yard, the relevant cards are collected together and suitable waybills added. These might say 'Goods shed' or 'Cattle Dock', for example. When it arrives at its destination, the operator uses the waybills to shunt the wagons to their correct locations.

Such systems are ideal for operating at home but not very convenient at exhibitions where they would inevitably slow down proceedings.

CHAPTER EIGHT

OPERATING AT EXHIBITIONS

Many people enjoy operating their model railways at home and there are many famous layouts, from 'Buckingham' to 'North Shields' that do not normally go to shows, but in Britain the majority of the hobby revolves around exhibitions. This is a mixed blessing; taking your layout to a model railway show is a very enjoyable experience and it is a great way to make friends. But it also creates a conflict in the mind of operators between the desire to operate realistically and yet keep the public entertained.

Bob Essery tells a story of when the North London Group of the Scalefour Society first exhibited their famous layout 'Heckmondwike'. They were operating correctly with signalmen sending bell codes and drivers driving trains, just like the real thing, and they were also pausing between a train being accepted by the signalman and the driver starting the train to create the illusion that the train was travelling through the block section. But the public complained that "the bells ring, but the trains don't run"! If you observed trains at a through station like 'Heckmondwike' in real life, there would be a considerable gap between train movements, but at exhibitions this is not deemed acceptable.

A compromise is clearly required where some sort of movement is always taking place to keep the public entertained, with movements taking place in a slow and purposeful way. For example, on 'Eccleston' we aim to keep some shunting going on in the goods yard most of the time in between the arrival and departure of passenger trains.

It also helps to operate to a timetable and to display that timetable to the public in some form. That way at least the viewers have an idea of what is going on and can anticipate the next planned movement. Various systems using index cards and other paper-based ways of displaying timetables have been used over the years and these days computers are coming into their own and being used to display such information. This is something I have yet to tackle with my own layout but it is on the 'To Do' list!

As I mentioned in the chapter on signalling, the use of block bells and instruments to communicate between operators eliminates the need for operators to shout at each other behind the layout and is a much more railwaylike approach.

Calderwood is a superb finescale 00 layout built by John Dilnot and Dave Kirby depicting a station on the L&YR's main line through the Calder Valley in Pre-Grouping days. Here an Aspinall 0-8-0 heads a 'Right Away Goods' consisting of butter vans along the main line while an Aspinall 0-6-0ST waits in the Goods Loop with a Merchandise train.
AUTHOR

A busy scene on the S7 layout at 'Ellerton Road': on the left a Midland Railway 0-4-4T stands at the platform with a passenger train while in the goods yard a Midland 0-6-0 is shunting a rake of mineral wagons destined for the gasworks.
EMMA HAYWOOD

L&YR Aspinall 0-6-0 No. 1028 arrives at Eccleston with a Through Goods from Lostock Hall.   SIMON EDMUNDS

Having run-round its train and disposed of the brake van, the loco has shunted its train into the goods yard.
SIMON EDMUNDS

If possible, the operating team should get together with the layout before a show and practise running the timetable. Not only does this familiarise everyone with the sequence, but it also enables people to practise in each operating position, and it has the added advantage of finding snags before the show itself.

A couple of years ago the lovely S7 layout 'Ellerton Road' won four prizes at the Nottingham exhibition; two were for buildings but the other two were for 'Most authentically operated layout' and 'Most entertaining layout'. The latter was voted for by the visiting public and is proof that a layout which is operated in an authentic manner can also be entertaining.

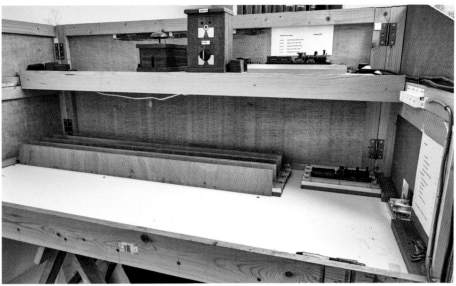

The Fiddle Yard at Eccleston showing the train and loco cassettes and the block instrument shelf.
SIMON EDMUNDS

Barton Wright 0-6-0 No. 952 shunts the vegetable warehouse sidings at Eccleston.   SIMON EDMUNDS

Frizinghall station, on the line between Shipley and Bradford, sometime in the 1950s, with 4F 0-6-0 No. 44216 shunting the yard.   R. S. CARPENTER COLLECTION

CONCLUSION

I hope you have enjoyed reading this book and found it useful. If it encourages more modellers to think about putting authentic operation at the heart of their hobby then I shall be very pleased.

To sum up:
- Think about the sort of traffic your model railway would convey
- Use a prototype trackplan or devise one that follows the practice of your chosen prototype
- Use working signals to control the trains and bells and block instruments for communication between operators
- Use a prototype Working Timetable or devise one that follows prototype practice
- Use a prototype Rule Book or devise some rules and regulations for the way you want your layout to work
- Use correct train formations for your chosen prototype and era
- Run your trains realistically and pause between movements

If you do some or all of this, I am sure you will agree with me that operating your layout authentically is fun and will greatly enhance your enjoyment of our wonderful hobby.

BIBLIOGRAPHY

General railway history
Fire and Steam by Christian Wolmar, Alantic Books, 2007

Railway accidents
Red for Danger by L. T. C. Rolt, David Charles, 1966

Model railway operation
Model Railway Operation by C. J. Freezer, PSL, 1993
The Living Model Railway by Robert Powell Hendry, Silver Link, 1994
Modelling Historic Railways by David Jenkinson, PSL, 1985
Historical Railway Modelling by David Jenkinson, Pendragon, 2001
Model Railway Operation by Frank Dyer, a series of articles in *Model Railway Journal* Nos. 27, 30-36 & 42

Prototype railway operation
Railway Operation for the Modeller by Bob Essery, Ian Allan, 2003
Passenger Train Operation for the Railway Modeller by Bob Essery, Ian Allan, 2005
Freight Train Operation for the Railway Modeller by Bob Essery, Ian Allan, 2006
Train Shunting and Marshalling for the Modeller by Bob Essery, Ian Allan, 2011

Track Plans
An Historical Survey of Selected LMS Stations (Two volumes) by Dr. R. Preston Hendry and R. Powell Hendry, OPC 1982 and 1986
An Historical Survey of The Midland in Gloucestershire by Peter Smith, OPC
An Historical Survey of the Chester to Holyhead Railway by V. R. Anderson and G. K. Fox, OPC
An Historical Survey of The Didcot, Newbury and Southampton Railway by C. W. Judge, OPC
An Historical Survey of The Somerset and Dorset Railway by C. W. Judge and C. R. Potts, OPC

Stations and Structures of the Settle & Carlisle Railway by V. R. Anderson and G. K. Fox, OPC
Rails in the Fells by David Jenkinson, Peco
Track Layouts of the GWR and BR (WR) by R. A. Cooke
Through Limestone Hills by Bill Hudson, OPC

Signalling
Model Railway Signalling by C. J. Freezer, PSL, 1991
Railway Signalling and Track Plans by Bob Essery, Ian Allan, 2007
British Railway Signalling by G. M. Kichenside and Alan Williams, Ian Allan, 1963
Signalling in the Age of Steam by Michael A. Vanns, Ian Allan
A Pictorial Record of LNWR Signalling by Richard D. Foster, OPC, 1982
A Pictorial Record of LNER Constituent Signalling by A. A. Maclean, OPC, 1983
A Pictorial Record of Southern Signals by G. Pryer, OPC, 1977
A Pictorial Record of Great Western Signalling by A. Vaughan, OPC, 1973
A Pictorial Record of LMS Signals by L. G. Warburton and V. R. Anderson, OPC, 1972
The Signalbox by The Signalling Study Group, OPC, 1986
Mechanical Railway Signalling by H. Raynar Wilson, 1904, Signalling Record Society
Signalboxes by Michael A. Vanns, Ian Allan, 1997
An Illustrated History of Signalling by Michael A. Vanns, Ian Allan, 1997
Two Centuries of Railway Signalling by Geoffrey Kichenside and Alan Williams, OPC, 1998

SOURCES OF INFORMATION
The Historical Model Railway Society (*www.hmrs.orog.uk*). They can provide contact details for all line societies.
The National Railway Museum, York (*www.nrm.org.uk*)
The National Archives, Kew (*www.nationalarchives.gov.uk*)
The Signalling Record Society (*www.s-r-s.org.uk*)

Acknowledgements
I would like to thank John Thompson and Jim Summers for giving me their comments on my draft text, Steve Hall for his contribution to the chapter on timetables, Tim Venton for his help with the chapter on rules and regulations, Simon Edmunds for photographing my layout, Barry Luck for photographing his layout 'Plumpton Green', Roger Mellor and Mike Fitton for giving me permission to use photographs and drawings from the L&YRS Collection, and Paul Karau for turning my prose into this book. One of the great joys of this hobby is the friendships you make along the way and over the years I have made many friends, both through my modelling activities and through my involvement with The Lancashire & Yorkshire Railway Society. They are too numerous to mention them all here, however they know who they are and I would like to thank them all for their friendship, support, help and encouragement. If you would like to know more about The Lancashire & Yorkshire Railway and the Society, please visit our website *www.lyrs.org.uk*.